POETRY CO~

GREAT MINDS

Your World...Your Future...YOUR WORDS

From Belfast

Edited by Steve Twelvetree

 Young**Writers**

First published in Great Britain in 2005 by:
Young Writers
Remus House
Coltsfoot Drive
Peterborough
PE2 9JX
Telephone: 01733 890066
Website: www.youngwriters.co.uk

SB ISBN 1 84460 716 X

Foreword

This year, the Young Writers' 'Great Minds' competition proudly presents a showcase of the best poetic talent selected from over 40,000 up-and-coming writers nationwide.

Young Writers was established in 1991 to promote the reading and writing of poetry within schools and to the youth of today. Our books nurture and inspire confidence in the ability of young writers and provide a snapshot of poems written in schools and at home by budding poets of the future.

The thought, effort, imagination and hard work put into each poem impressed us all and the task of selecting poems was a difficult but nevertheless enjoyable experience.

We hope you are as pleased as we are with the final selection and that you and your family continue to be entertained with *Great Minds From Belfast* for many years to come.

Contents

Jamie Shaw (13)	49
Nathan Gilbert (13)	49
Alan Graham (14)	50
David Beattie (13)	50
Neil Allen (14)	51
Jonathan Beckett (13)	51
Henry Milne (12)	52
Ryan Miskelly (14)	52
Kriss Brown (13)	52
Wade Aitken (13)	53
Samuel Crothers (13)	53
David Wilton (13)	54
Lee Carson (14)	54
Ross McGivern (13)	55
Laurie Caruth (14)	55
Ben Dinnen (14)	56
Robert Black (12)	56
Steven McLean (12)	57
Tafozzul Haque (12)	57
Mark Higgins (14)	58
Rory Coalter (12)	58
Philip McBride (12)	59
Jack Moore (14)	59
David McLearnon (13)	60
Curtis Howe (12)	60
Jonathan Thompson (12)	61
Aaron Clarke (11)	61
Christopher Blacker (12)	62
Jackson Hutchinson (12)	62
Stephen Rooney (14)	63
Dale Lockhart (13)	64
Raymond Algie (14)	64
Christopher Kemp (13)	65
Jordyn Ralston (12)	65
Adam Shanley (13)	66
Matthew Hamilton (14)	66
Johnathon Pavis (13)	67
John Williams (12)	67
David Nesbitt (15)	68
Ryan McCoy (12)	68
Christopher Nelson (16)	69
Nicky Telford (12)	69

Chris Tollerton (12)	70
Adam Dickinson (13)	70
Kingsley Davidson (12)	71
Ben Uprichard (12)	71
Curtis Spence (14)	72
Geoffrey Atkinson (12)	72
Stephen Magill (12)	73
Jonathan Sheil (14)	73
Ross McMillan (12)	74
Jonathan Dalzell (11)	74
Christopher Walker (13)	74
Ryan Hill (11)	75
Michael McMillan (11)	75
Stephen Hamilton (11)	75
Laurence Boyle (14)	76
Jamie Edgar (12)	76
Curtis Adams (12)	77
Adam Suitor (14)	77
David Tipping (12)	77
Neil Butler (13)	78
Rian Budde (11)	78
Matthew Hicks (13)	79
Lee Thompson (11)	79
Chris Rafferty (13)	80
Jonathan McCaughan (13)	80
Andrew Rooney (11)	81
Craig Holmes (13)	81
Richard Lewis (11)	82
Ryan Stirling (12)	82
Michael Carey (11)	83
Andrew Steed (15)	84
Mark Irvine (11)	84
Bradley Dodds (11)	85
David Docherty (11)	85
Andrew Ellison (15)	86
Ryan Tate (15)	86
Daryl Finlay (11)	87
Michael Sewell (13)	87
Kyle Young (12)	88
Nathan Dickson (15)	88
Gerald Taulo (11)	89
Matthew Wightman (11)	89

Matthew Brown (12)	90
Daniel Mills (13)	90
Stuart Campton (13)	91
Jamie Reid (12)	92
Mark Watty (13)	92
Christopher McDowell (13)	93
Steven Browne (13)	93
Graeme Stevenson (14)	94
Matthew Tipping (13)	94
Joshua Smyth (12)	95
David Hodson (11)	95
Chris Boyd (14)	96
Kristian Bloomer (11)	96
Martyn Cummings (14)	97
Mark McCann (11)	97
Robert Douglas (14)	98
Ryan Hamilton (11)	98
Simon Laverty (11)	99
David Stewart (13)	100
Phillip Cooke (11)	100
Raymond McClure (14)	101
Stephen McConnell (11)	101
Roger Meaklim (14)	102
Kyle McGarvey (11)	102
David Quinn (13)	103
Reece Shaw (11)	103
Craig Campbell (13)	104
Colin Turnbull (12)	104
David Atkinson (13)	105
Andrew Mundy (12)	105
James Malcolm (13)	106
James Wright (12)	106
Ben Houston (12)	107
Adam Letson (13)	107
Jonathon Bowden (12)	108
Andrew Gilmour (12)	108
Darren Bingham (15)	109
Michael Bush (13)	109
Dean Kerrigan (13)	110
Karl Hutton (12)	110
Wayne Clarke (13)	111
Luke McCall (14)	111

Jason McCann (15)	135
Michael McClean (15)	135
Andrew Hunter (15)	136
Jack Stewart (12)	137
Lewis Cameron (15)	138
Matthew Perry (12)	138
Gareth Brown (12)	139
Jonathon McIlfatrick (12)	139
Ben Watton (12)	140
Gareth Murray (15)	140
Robert McCaughan (15)	141
Corey Watson (12)	142
Adam Turnbull (12)	142
Jamie Laurie (12)	143
Wayne Carson (12)	143
Michael Adams (12)	144
Kenneth Comfort (14)	144

Belfast Model School For Girls
Naomi Gray (11)	145

Bloomfield Collegiate
Charlotte Howard (11)	145
Sarah Davey (12)	146
Lisa Parr (11)	147
Jodi Doherty (12)	147
Melanie Gibson (12)	148
Elizabeth Peace (14)	148
Amanda Watterson (12)	149
Norah Officer (11)	149
Nicola Shepherd (11)	150
Rachel Martin (12)	150
Chloe Lynas (12)	151
Rebecca Lucas (12)	151
Lisa Hollywood (13)	152
Victoria Scott (13)	153
Rebekah Robinson (13)	154
Janet Martin (12)	155
Natasha Gunning (13)	156
Nicola Black (13)	157
Jennifer McKee (12)	158

Ben Lowry (12)	205
Hee Jin Cho (14)	206
Ciara McGlade (12)	207
Eimeár McGarry (15)	208
Morgan MacIntyre (12)	208
Juliet Stirling (13)	209
Maurizio Liberante (11)	209
Kirsty Kee (12)	210
Adam Irwin (12)	211
Jonathan Stanfield (13)	212
Nathan Jun (13)	213
Kym Irwin (12)	214
Lorna Hamilton (12)	215
Elizabeth Crooks (13)	216
Adam Carr (11)	216
Connell Stewart (12)	217
Brajith Srigengan (13)	218
Steve Heagney (15)	218
Helen Moore (15)	219
Emily Cheung (12)	219
Graham Richardson (16)	220
Alanna Holmes (11)	220
Mark McCauley (16)	221
Rachel Watters (12)	221
Holly Graham (11)	222
Philip Stewart (12)	222
Oliver Dickson (11)	222
Olivia Lowry (11)	223
Karl Hudson (11)	223
Conor Cathcart (11)	223
Conner Gallagher (12)	224

Orangefield High School

Danielle Martin (13)	224
Sarah-Louise McLaughlin (12)	225
Adam Bradford (13)	225
Wayne Brown (12)	225
Cory McCaw (13)	226
Aaron Ashton (12)	226
Leah Reid (14)	227
John Miller (14)	227

Our Lady Of Mercy Girls' School

The Poems

My Baboon!

Shall I compare thee to the midnight moon?
No, thy ist more like a baboon!
Your long, wild and matted hair
Greets me every morning with a red-eyed stare
Whenever your hunger doth hit
I always have to beat you off with my Hurley stick
Whenever the baby gets in your way
He takes one look at you and runs like startled prey
When you talk it's more often a scream
Knowing you'll create a big scene!
So when we do venture out
Everybody about
Makes a dash
Like they've been offered some of my dad's mash!

Sharon Doherty   (16)
Aquinas Diocesan Grammar School

Frys

Bob was a guy,
Who liked a good fry.
It's been twenty years now,
And his hips are as wide as a ship's bow.
He's been told time and time again,
Keep eatin' them things and you'll end up with a cane.
Bob didn't care,
Even when they gave him the stare.
Quit eatin' them things,
Or you'll end up like your great aunt Bing.
But Bob just kept walkin' on,
Prayin' for his poor aunt when gone.
Bob isn't with us anymore . . .
He slipped and hit his head on the floor.

Michael Malanaphy (14)
Aquinas Diocesan Grammar School

Tick-Tock, Tick-Tock

White in the face
About to cry
I pull myself together and
Hide behind a broken smile

My great granny's ill
She is in the theatre
So we all go home
And sit and stare at the clock

Tick-tock, tick-tock
Never let the clock stop
When it does
She will be gone

They cry and make jokes
Hoping they will cheer everyone up
I take my sister and cousin into a different room
To leave the adults to talk

They are worried
They are angry
You can see it in their eyes
It's like watching volcanoes erupt

Tick-tock, tick-tock
The clock is stopping
When it does
She will be gone

We decide to go to the hospital
My mother tells me it will be upsetting
So I stay and later
The phone it rings

When I answer it
I'm full of fear
And from my eyes
Fall a thousand tears

Tick-tock, tick-tock
Five minutes ago
The clock it stopped
RIP, she's gone.

Sarah Thompson (13)
Aquinas Diocesan Grammar School

Whether You Like It Or Not

I heard the exciting music of the film I was watching,
A whisper from the sofa made me turn around.
Mum and Dad were sitting there looking . . .
Almost guilty?

'We're going to have a baby.'
And in that moment my world fell apart
And I burst into tears.
I was afraid, but didn't know why.

In school we're talking about the 11+,
That's coming in November.
I see everybody so normal -
Need to get everything off my chest.

I feel, rather than see the smirks
And whispers behind my back,
After the mask of their congratulations,
All because of my mum's age.

The big day came,
And on the 17th April I held him for the first time,
My wee brother Luca.

Marisa McVey (12)
Aquinas Diocesan Grammar School

Wayne Rooney

Wayne Rooney; what a guy
He loves a steak and kidney pie

He looks like Shrek with his chubby face
But he definitely isn't short of pace

What a talent - he's only eighteen
His goal scoring rate is pretty mean

His strength scares defenders a bit
When he has to, he uses his grit

He used to play in Merseyside
When he asked to quit, David Moyes nearly died

Since joining United he's lit up the crowd
I'm sure his old man would be very proud

He likes the women, it's plain to see
He's better than you - maybe even me.

Conor Cunningham (14)
Aquinas Diocesan Grammar School

Ms Johnstone

Ms Johnstone trying her best,
All the kids making a mess,
She works for very little pay,
To try and get her through the day,
Although it breaks this mother's heart,
Her twins must always be apart,
This mother tries to sit and rest,
But she knows the separation was for the best,
She dreams for a better life for them,
But this doesn't work out in the end.

Paul McAleer (15)
Aquinas Diocesan Grammar School

Reflections In The Mirror

Everywhere you go there are mirrors,
Mirrors in the cold ice,
In a murky puddle of rain lying on the ground,
In a newly cleaned window,
A mirror in the bathroom and the one hanging in the hall,
A cracked mirror hidden from view as it will bring seven years
                                                    of bad luck.

Mirrors showing reflections,
So clear that you feel you can put your hand through their surface
Into a new, distant land somewhere,
A cold place, with no feelings, just images.
Where every word is backwards
srdawkcab si drow yreve erehW.

Where left is right and right turns to left,
A reflection shows us everything.
How we look on the outside,
But that's all a reflection can ever show.
The outside of a person, the exterior of a place,
The superficial view.

It makes you wonder how we spend so much time looking
                                            into their depths.
Striving for perfection when the person who we see reflected,
Isn't who we want to see staring back at us.
Why do we care what we see?
The one thing that the mirror can never reflect is personality.
Colourfulness of a person, the real you,
More than just a reflection in a mirror.

Deirdre McKeown (15)
Aquinas Diocesan Grammar School

My Faithful Feline Friend

I hear her breath, her purr
I feel her coat, her fur
I open my eyes, I smile.

First light, a new day dawns
She stretches, she scratches, she yawns
I close my eyes, I smile.

She is there for me always
Through dark and gloomy days
I think of her, I smile.

Maeve McGreevy (14)
Aquinas Diocesan Grammar School

The Troublesome Boy

There was a boy from Dublin,
Who really loved troublin'.
He'd punch your face,
Untie your lace,
Until you went a tumblin'!

Emma Hughes (14)
Aquinas Diocesan Grammar School

Do It Wrong All Along

Write a colourful picture,
Or draw a catchy song.
Sing an exciting story,
Or do it wrong all along.

Dance to a really high mountain,
Or climb a catchy song.
Or you know what you could really do,
You could do it along all wrong.

Chris Heaney (14)
Aquinas Diocesan Grammar School

Our World

Look at our beautiful world,
So fresh and new.
Until the day comes when men
Cut our forests down and
Kill a lot of animals.
They pollute our air and waters,
And the worst thing is knowing
We've done it too,
Just by throwing a piece of
Rubbish on the ground, or
Sticking chewing gum under a table.
That is the thing that makes me sad,
But me stopping doing all that stuff
Doesn't mean the world
Is going to stop with me.

Louise Madden (12)
Aquinas Diocesan Grammar School

The Sorrow Of My Eternal Love

Shall I compare thee to a web of lies?
Thou art more devious and intimidating,
When thou looked beyond me to the clear skies,
And when thou asked of my debating
Thou spokes not of old archaic,
And I would not be left in the dark,
And I was left to stare at your mosaic,
And so I will make the final remark,
But do not fret of my sudden return,
Nor lose sleep over my eternal coup,
Nor serve attention to my dear concerns,
For it is your air that is left 'true blue',
And you will know that my name is the Lord,
When you are the one who receives no award.

Paul Sloan (15)
Aquinas Diocesan Grammar School

An Autumn's Leaf

Shall I compare thee to an autumn's leaf?
Thou art more delicate of your exterior
Sharp rain does fall during they season underneath
And autumn's colours all too bright for they interior
Sometimes too often an autumn leaf may fall
And diminishes the beauty of your difference
And to compare thee I should not recall
Though the rain of autumn soon does rinse
But thy eternal rain does not dry
Nor thy interior change its ways
Nor shall time make thee cry
For when it's written it shall live through the days
So long as the seasons do pass
The beauty remains of what thee has.

Leah Despard (15)
Aquinas Diocesan Grammar School

Mrs Johnstone

All the kids making a mess,
poor Mrs Johnstone trying her best.
Cleaning the houses night and day,
struggling to get a bit of pay.
She can hardly manage with the ones she's got,
another two will be an awful lot.

She brings up all her children well,
all her things she has to sell.
She doesn't let the poverty show,
yet she tries her best to bring home the dough.
Thinking about the two new ones,
will there ever be enough funds?

Michael Loughan (14)
Aquinas Diocesan Grammar School

A Mouse In The Grass

Shall I compare thee to a mouse in the grass?
With thy quiet innocence and furried glint,
Thy trailing blazer tail and shoes like glass,
As down the long pathway you lost boys sprint.
Don't feel like food, but there's the bell,
Just line up for dinner without a fuss.
Noses twitching in the noise and smell,
No worries now for soon comes home time bus.
Thy organising power will never fail,
And thy clever mind cannot forget,
Prepared for all, come snow or hail
And to all thy teachers don't be in debt.
Never count on me for a helping hand,
For alone too was I, you must understand.

Helen McGourty (16)
Aquinas Diocesan Grammar School

An Ode To Anna

Shall I compare thee to a bonbon?
More contrasted and deep throughout
Although sometimes your sweetness can be a con,
But you're just as sweet I have no doubt,
With enclosed bitter pain.
To tempt you too fast
With all of your beauty you become vain,
But with time of softening this will not last
Depending on time you become grim.
Of the harm you will do I do not know the truth
Taking all this I'd miss you like a limb
But with your temptress ways you attract a sweet tooth,
You stick to me like a toffee to my teeth
If you were to leave I would sustain grief.

Nainsi Best (15)
Aquinas Diocesan Grammar School

Shall I Compare Thee To A Forbidden Something?

Shall I compare thee to a forbidden something?
Seeing you around and knowing you can't be mine
Although nothing compares to the happiness you bring,
Everything I feel, I have to push aside
I lie awake and try so hard not to think of you
But I can't help it, you're in my dreams
Who can decide what they dream? And dream I do
I don't even know what this all means
It's selfish to only think of me
I know I shouldn't feel this way
But I'm not going to just sit and cry
I just want to see you, and want to say
For always and eternity,
You will mean the world to me.

Hayley Eastwood (15)
Aquinas Diocesan Grammar School

Shall I Compare Thee To A Rose On Snow?

Shall I compare thee to a rose on snow?
Like you it's beautiful and delicate.
The snow sparkles like your eyes, you know,
It shines like your smile, no one could hate.
But the rose's end won't come too late -
The snow will melt, the rose will die,
You shall not share the rose's fate,
It's gone, forgotten, lost with time,
This won't happen to you - I'll tell everyone
How your beauty far exceeds the rose,
A tribute to you, this verse shall become,
The ages will hear of your perfect nose!
When we're gone, this will last, for all to see,
Forever, eternal, in this poem for thee.

Anna Mulvenna (16)
Aquinas Diocesan Grammar School

Finest Lamb Chop

Shall I compare thee to a lamb chop?
Thou art more tasteful than sweetcorn and peas
Beauty and taste with thy gravy on top,
And thy hot yams stay warm long
Sometime thou art wonder what to drink
So thou should have wine that is sweet and strong
Thy beauty starts making me think
How does thou make his love be felt
As I embrace and consume thy tender meat
Like thy sweet potatoes on top the butter does melt
All but so tender, loving and sweet
And as I look upon thy empty plate
Thou does not fear for thy food will be there for some time
And just like this food, thou art mine.

Martin McManus (16)
Aquinas Diocesan Grammar School

A Sonnet For You?

You think that this sonnet is about you
Sorry, but you're just not that inspiring,
Maybe that was harsh, you know you are cool,
But you just don't consume my admiring.
You're so vain, a pain in my brain, explain!
The devotion of one less boy won't hurt.
But lack of attention drives you insane,
Don't think you'll get it with a shorter skirt!
Was it a law that I'd fall at your feet?
A helpless devotee joining the fleet?
You think magazines are where you belong,
Sounds like the girl from that Mike Skinner song.
'Fit But You Know It' is the name of the tune,
You probably think it's about you too.

John D'Arcy (15)
Aquinas Diocesan Grammar School

Deep Hatred

Can I detest you every day and night?
Thou art so hated, unloved and unclean,
May we never meet on each other's site,
The biggest boar I have ever seen!
Hated like the rain that falls in summer
And all the splinters found in my oak chair,
Like the beating from a crazy drummer,
By chance I hope you know that I don't care!
Your face will always be unwelcome here,
Like death I hate you, no matter what day
I curse the day you called me 'little dear'
I take no heed at all of what you say!
My feelings are easily clear to see
My feelings are of deep hatred to thee!

Caitriona Reilly (15)
Aquinas Diocesan Grammar School

My Rusty Old Bike

Shall I compare thee to a brand new bike?
Thou art more smoother and more cooler.
My friend is a mechanic known as Mike,
He will fix you when you are broken.
Even though you do need fuel to go,
It cannot go as fast as you can.
And I just want to let you know,
You make me a really happy man,
And on that day you had broken down,
I had to go and get you repaired.
It had cost me quite a few pounds.
I got you a new seat from the one that was torn.
You will always be fixed again,
So you will not always be in pain.

Kevin Wilkinson (16)
Aquinas Diocesan Grammar School

A Rose Petal

Shall I compare thee with a rose petal,
Or does thou prefer the morrow's pink dawn?
You, are as beautiful as kings' gold metal,
And also are as full of life as a fawn.
Thou deserves more worth than palace or tower,
A sea wind, chill while unbidden and brief
Yet real, a quest any knight would travel far.
Thou won't die, eternal, no rose, nor leaf,
But we fear thou art not what thee seems -
For what seems bejewelled is a snake with no care.
And thee will not preserve, is what we deem,
One is decrepit, that I fear, from fair,
Halt! Let concepts remain in the pitch dark,
And my memory of you remain stark.

Azwan Isa (16)
Aquinas Diocesan Grammar School

Shall I Compare Thee To A Chocolate Bar?

Shall I compare thee to a chocolate bar?
Thou art more pleasing to the eye,
And to seek your love, I never travel far
For to be in your presence I need not buy.
You will always be close at hand to me
Everyone is free to share your beauty
Each time I see you I don't pay a fee.
And to spend your love is my one duty.
But when everything has been devoured,
And nothing is left but paper covering,
I know it's not the end, and won't be hard
I know I'll see you at our next meeting.
And once again you can shine upon me,
And once again, happy I shall then be.

Éadaoin Devlin (16)
Aquinas Diocesan Grammar School

All She Needs

All she needs is an outstretched hand,
A voice that tells her that they understand,
A smile to wash her tears away
And make her hopeful for the coming day.

All she needs is a loving heart
To make sure she doesn't fall apart,
And when she wakes up in the middle of the night,
To have somebody who'll hold her tight.

All she needs is a goodnight kiss,
And a look to show that she'll be sorely missed.
All she needs is someone to be true
And to whisper the words, 'I love you'.

But nobody cares about what she needs
Because eyes are blinded with the sin of greed.
All she has are the stars of night
To wish upon, that everything will be alright.

Laura Dornan (14)
Aquinas Diocesan Grammar School

Shall I Compare Thee To A Mobile Phone?

Shall I compare thee to a mobile phone?
Thou art more versatile and melodic
Much traffic doth weaken the signal received
And obsolescence doth come with too much haste
The name of caller I do sometimes ignore
Or answering I sigh in words do waste
With every bill expense doth seem to rise
For talk or text or photo, song revised
But thy soft voice is sweet and true your eyes
Nor shall thou fail to entertain or please
No contract, air-time text we need to bundle
Just living as we go, each day topped up
No fashion or renewal begs divest
Just love eternal from me to thee.

Moya McGurk (16)
Aquinas Diocesan Grammar School

All Night Long

Bang! Bang! Bang!
The noises never cease.
Boom! Boom! Boom!
The sounds continue. All night long.

People are crying,
People are dying,
Spirits are ascending,
Spirits are dying.

The morning's chaos says it all,
As men and women are all in despair.
I see a woman crying in sadness,
Holding an infant in her arms.
He isn't moving.

This barren land is nothing like home,
It is as hot as molten lava.
Not a plant, tree, flower or fruit within sight,
Nothing but the sight of death, despair and misfortune.

The smell of decay surrounds me,
It's the kiss of death.
A chill goes down my spine
As cold as the heart of Jack Frost.
At that moment, time paused.

Bang! Bang! Bang!
Bang! Bang! Bang!
Nooooooooo!
I have just left the building.

The men in suits claim it is over,
But that's far from the truth.
Bang! Bang! Bang!
Boom! Boom! Boom!
The sounds continue. All night long.

Oran Kennedy (13)
Aquinas Diocesan Grammar School

The Hospital Visit

I walked through those double doors
And along the spotless floors,
The nurses give me a friendly smile
The doctors next to me put sheets in a pile.

I walked up the stairs,
To my left is intensive care
To my right,
My granda's room, it is very bright.

He looked at me with a stare,
Which would have given anyone a scare.
In his room it smelt of lavender
And on the wall was a nice little calendar.

We stayed there for a while, and so,
We had to go,
Back through those double doors
And along the spotless floors.

Sarah McConville (13)
Aquinas Diocesan Grammar School

Be Positive

When night has come I'm sure that life is over.
As I see my love disappear from grasp.
I can't bear to think, he's gone forever.
As I fade behind bars, hidden by a mask.
To think of the happiness my love could bring,
As I lie in this jail, lonely, incomplete.
I remember my dreams that one day I'd wear his ring
And I'd dance like a queen as my life was fulfilled.
But suddenly, light comes behind those bars,
And summer sun shines through the glass.
A beautiful face, my love appears from afar.
The hope that has gone has now appeared.
Be positive as hope is always there,
It will guide you to freedom, always near.

Maria McGrath (15)
Aquinas Diocesan Grammar School

Mickey

Poor little Mickey living in the rough end of town,
Got his gun stolen by Sammy,
Who has a plate in his crown.
Seven kids in his family,
Mickey's one of the worst,
They say he's not going to Heaven
Because he knows how to curse.
He got in trouble with the police, you see,
That won't happen to me.
They chased him for putting a hole in someone's head,
He laughed and cheered with glee.
He's in jail now,
He's on the pills as well,
He found out he had a twin, so he shot him dead,
Now Mickey's the one with a hole in his head.

Conor Murray (15)
Aquinas Diocesan Grammar School

Remember The Stars

Shall I compare you to an autumn eve?
You are as dark and as mysterious,
The ground turns to gold when covered in leaves,
And stars do appear as night surrounds us.
Rain taps on my window sounding so mild,
Its tranquillity makes me feel the same,
As you do, and so I, just like a child,
Get a chill at every sound of your name.
But do you feel the same, much as I do?
My confusion of your ways tells me not.
Like autumn weather you have been untrue,
And the hurt you have caused, I have not forgot.
Though time will pass and we both will have changed,
I'll remember the stars, now and again.

Nuala Love (15)
Aquinas Diocesan Grammar School

The Ranger's Journey

Something is not right here,
Where is the taste of my beer?
Where is the glow of the sky?
Has the evercrystal begun to die?

I go to the king's tower, a glowing gem,
To see the king, obese and dim,
He accused me of theft, his voice grim,
But I never took it, the evercrystal I mean,
It's broken, stolen and I left for Turean.

In exile, I'm in now,
Still searching I am, but no luck anyhow,
Until a foul cave, a terrible moan,
I followed the sound to a final groan.

The crystal was there, untouched and repaired!
I tried to grab it, but to my despair,
A Fermellion, rotting and grey was in my path,
I unsheathed my sword and began to laugh,
A battle took place, long and hard,
Till I gave the final blow to that unearthly bollard.

I brought the crystal home to cheers and applause
And thanks for the home-bringing of the cause,
Of life and death, of health and pain,
This gem, is something my destiny made me gain.

May our country fall, be plagued or destroyed,
But our gem will rebuild our city again,
Rewrite history, diaries and books,
It will bring back what death took,
May crystal be holy, may crystal be strong,
Protect us and city all eternity long.

Niall Gallagher (12)
Aquinas Diocesan Grammar School

All Hallows Eve

Lost souls they roam around
In their everlasting doom
And werewolves they do howl
At the sight of a Hallowe'en moon.

Hear the cries of children
That died when they were young
Never ever again
Will they glimpse the sun.

Glance up at the sky
Darkness ever prevails
Huddle up inside
And bang up your door with nails.

For dangers lurk outside
I'm afraid they shall not leave
Until the darkness has passed that is
All Hallows Eve.

Eithne Fraser (11)
Aquinas Diocesan Grammar School

The Sea

Rolling and tumbling,
Tossing and turning,
Thrashing and howling,
Deep blues and foaming white.

It sounds like a banshee,
Screaming constantly,
It's like it's in pain,
Like a thousand two-year-olds yelling for food.

Its deep, murky depths,
Which no one dares to enter,
Waiting to swallow you up.

Maeve McQuillan (12)
Aquinas Diocesan Grammar School

That Awful Day

The phone was ringing,
I heard my mother crying
The tears that tore her heart.
I questioned, 'What's wrong? I have to know,
I must know, tell me.'

I walked down the street
After school, hoping he was all right.
What if I run away,
And when I come back he will be better?

His face was shocking,
I wanted to cry,
But I stayed strong for him.

People say forget about it,
But how can I? Can you answer that?
I want to cry,
But I will stay strong for him,
My brother.

Una Lavery (12)
Aquinas Diocesan Grammar School

My Poem On Quad Biking!

Anticipation:
Drip, drop, drip, drop
Gloom, boredom, patter, patter
Discovery, excitement, chatter
Dreading, pleading, swaying, awaying.

Exhilaration:
Vroom-vroom, vroom-vroom,
Vroom-vroom,
Wind blowing in our faces
Heads down for the races,
Hearts pounding, muck flying
David and I tying, tying!

Cara Breen (12)
Aquinas Diocesan Grammar School

The Match Of A Lifetime

Walking on that pitch
The whole world watching my back
Carrying the ball, I looked at
My teammates, my friends,
All as eager as me.

The whistle blew, oh so loud
Off I flew, hearing the crowd
After the opposing team.

I wasn't that great,
But I played my heart out.
Suddenly, the ball was at my feet,
This was my chance.

I was forward, looking for a man,
No one else was there to share the burden
But I saw the clock 89:40
This was it, I shot.

Niall Quinn (14)
Aquinas Diocesan Grammar School

Moving

We are moving again, what a surprise,
I could see the fear glisten in my mother's eyes.
Another attack, this time at three,
How many times are we going to be
Rejected by people, we thought were friends?

I used to think that it was about me
But now that I'm older I'm able to see
That it's about our religion.

It's down to a few different people believing
In different gods and races
That's why we're leaving.

Nicola Ferguson (13)
Aquinas Diocesan Grammar School

The 11th September 2001

On 11th September 2001
There came an event that made men run
And people would shudder from place to place
As the US stared terrorism in the face

For Osama bin Laden was an evil man
(And it is believed he fled to Afghanistan)
He had a horrific, evil notion
And set his wicked plan in motion

On 11th September 2001
There came an event that made men run
And people would shudder from place to place
As the US stared terrorism in the face

New York was a city in the US of A
And a hideous event took place there one autumn's day
For there were two buildings called the Twin Towers
They were the symbols of America's power

On 11th September two planes cut through the sky
Everyone aboard them doomed to die
That day, a day of many tears
A culmination of so many fears

On 11th September 2001
There came an event that made men run
And people would shudder from place to place
As the US stared terrorism in the face

Into the buildings the planes came flying
On the ground, people were dying
So many drawing their final breath
One word on the air; that word was death

The most awful scene in US history
A scene that caused so many misery
Enter the firemen: New York's best
Many of whom would go to eternal rest

On 11th September 2001
There came an event that made men run
And people would shudder from place to place
As the US stared terrorism in the face

The brave firefighters gave up their lives
So many leaving distraught girlfriends and wives
A single sunrise, one sunset
Within that, a thousand people Death's shadow met

So many people, so many dead
Never again to return to their bed
For ere long, collapse did those towers
To shatter America's symbol of power

On 11th September 2001
There came an event that made men run
And people would shudder from place to place
As the US stared terrorism in the face

Mere hours later, then set the sun
On 11th September 2001
A dreadful day of sorrows passed
Another dark day in America's past

But in the end, bin Laden won not
Despite the sorrows he had wrought
For America now has a new symbol of power
And its name is Freedom Tower.

Kevin Feeney (13)
Aquinas Diocesan Grammar School

Mourn For Someone You Never Loved

At night he cries himself to sleep
All alone in the dark.
In school she walks past and
He can say nothing.
He pours his heart out to his best friend
And he can say nothing.

Trouble comes and trouble goes
But she will never leave his heart.
Sad, tormented by her,
He is alone for the last time.

Rebekah O'Neill (13)
Aquinas Diocesan Grammar School

The Gingerbread Men

I waited and waited while my mother made the pastry,
Finally they were put into the oven,
They looked oh so tasty.

They came out on a metal tray,
They were hot and the smell of baking wafted to my nose,
They looked oh so tasty.

I watched as my mum inscribed
The face and buttons on their chests,
They looked oh so tasty.

Even though I longed to eat them,
I was unsettled as they looked almost human, but,
They looked oh so tasty.

I grabbed one of their ginger legs,
And bit into the head,
They tasted oh so tasty.

The icing oozed into my mouth,
And they were so lovely,
They tasted oh so tasty.

In my head, I imagined them coming alive
And seeking vengeance against me for their headless brother
And they hit me, but not so hard.

Their icing bullets struck my chest,
They felt like snowdrops falling from the sky
And they hit me, but not so hard.

But this was only a dream,
And I ate my gingerbread men.
They tasted oh so tasty.

Eugene McQuaid (12)
Aquinas Diocesan Grammar School

War Hero

Do it for your country
And the benefit of Man.
Do it for your leader's thirst,
For power in his hands.

Do it for the honourable death
The honourable, piercing cries.
Oh yes, the honour in soldier children,
Who gave their life to lies.

Crippled by propaganda,
You now have no further use.
Thrown on a hidden plane,
Your pain given no excuse.

And now you sit at home,
With a paranoid, broken mind.
Tormented by the horror,
You tried to leave behind.

Ghostly images fill your days
And pleading screams your night.
The more you try to block it out,
The more it runs your life.

Disbelief swims round your thoughts,
Guilt seeps to your very core.
As you try to comprehend,
The casualties of war.

Scrub until you're raw,
But the blood on your hands won't wash away,
For you sold your soul to the Devil,
On the battlefields that day.

Lisa Marie Heaney (15)
Aquinas Diocesan Grammar School

Summer Exams

Every year,
We sit here like lampless moths.
Taken from the sun and warmth
To sit in this dingy classroom
For the end-of-year torture sessions.

Our brains decay
As we struggle to remember
Which verbs are 'or' and which are 'ar'?
And why on earth is there an accent in 'fatal'?
Or was I too busy counting my nose and
Dreaming about watching paint dry, to pay attention?

Every year,
We study and revise and study and revise for weeks.
Taken from the sun outside
To sit in this dingy classroom,
Only to forget everything.

Thank God I don't do French
And I manage to steal an hour
To look out of the back window and
Imagine the cool breeze, the summer warmth,
And the smell of freshly cut grass.
Instead, I am stuck here in this stuffy, smelly classroom
With not one window open so I can breathe.
And there goes the bell and we are free for ten minutes.

Every year,
We look forward to the end of our exams,
When we can untuck our shirts and
Eat all the ice cream we can get with two pounds.
We are taken from the sun outside for one last time,
To sit in this dingy classroom
And sit our last exam.

Finally, the last exam of all.
It's not hard, but still a struggle,
Especially with the sound of the ice cream van at the gate,
And the sun burning the back of my neck.

This exam is as boring as library period
But I still soldier on.
I almost fall asleep but the teacher's looking my way.
I attempt to finish my paper and then turn my attention to the clock.
Five seconds to go, not long now, *and there's the bell!*
We're free at last! Free for the summer -
But wait, there's still a week of school left! *Why, God, why?*

Deirdre Canavan (12)
Aquinas Diocesan Grammar School

Home

We drive up the untended mountain road in a rusty white van
Passing tin shacks looking abandoned, but home for some.
Arriving, we transfer to a black Land Rover for our rough journey
Through the muddy, humid and ongoing Indonesian rainforest,
Home to so many tribes and dangerous wildlife.
We reach our destination soon, but dark is near and lots to do.

I never thought I would meet a tribe, yet alone one's family.
Sharp eyes for hunting food and
Lean, tall, nimble bodies and hands for all their work.

We wash and play in the local river
Before having a hunted deer and rice for dinner.

I thought sleeping in a longhouse would be scary and hard so young,
But I realised all these people were like me.

Midnight,
Time for bed.
Generator off,
Complete darkness.

I lie there on the hard, uneven, wooden floor, all silent,
But the wildlife near,
Their sounds flooding my ears.

I wake, although never really asleep at all.
I see nothing, but I know everyone is there, safe.

Jeri Cronin (12)
Aquinas Diocesan Grammar School

Shark!

It was a nice sunny day on Owey Island
It was peaceful until:

I suddenly heard shouts,
I was curious, what was happening?
I ran outside to see.
I heard the words, 'Shark, on the beach!'

I ran to the beach as fast as I could,
My heart was beating with excitement.
Shark, a shark on the beach, ran through my head.
I had never seen a shark before!

I was as weak as water when I saw it.
I stood mesmerised by its size.
Suddenly fear hit me like a stone.
Could this thing come into the quay that we swam in?

It was obvious that it was carnivorous
As it was munching a shoal of mackerel!
I looked through a pair of my cousin's binoculars.
It was 25ft or more and could easily eat a man.

Most of my cousins had turned up.
We watched, entranced by its swimming.
After 15 minutes it swam away,
Off into the horizon.

Diarmuid Cowan (12)
Aquinas Diocesan Grammar School

The Day

As I walked out the sun looked down on me
With extreme heat, it looked as if it was angry.
It glared behind a hedge at everything that went by.
I looked up and it was walking behind the hills.
Then it began to run and it disappeared behind the clouds.

Suddenly, it smiled again, night was beginning to fall.
The sun turned red and slowly bent down until it disappeared.

Ciaran Ashe (13)
Aquinas Diocesan Grammar School

Edinburgh

When I was in P7 our teachers all told us
That we could go to Edinburgh and I knew it was a must
We were all so excited, our faces filled with glee
And a million tiny butterflies all whooped inside of me.
We went to loads of meetings, where they told us what we'd do
This was going to be fantastic and wonderful, I knew.
Eventually we packed our bags and made to cross the sea
I'd never been to Scotland and wondered how it'd be.
On the first night of our arrival there was a disco
But someone broke their fingers and I was picked to go.
Four hours in the hospital and I was really bored
Our teacher tried to crack some jokes, all of which I ignored.
At 2 o'clock we made our way back to our hotel
I closed my eyes at once, I've never slept that well.
The next few days flew past so quick
And so we packed our bags again, this was the end of our school trip.
The journey home was also short
And eventually we could see Belfast port
It slowly became clearer
As we drew slowly nearer.

Meadhbh Schaible (13)
Aquinas Diocesan Grammar School

Autumn Leaves Are Falling

Autumn leaves are yellow, red, brown and golden,
They swirl and twirl all around.
Eventually they fall like feathers to the ground.

The children's ardour to kick the leaves to make a crunching sound.
Animals hibernate, birds migrate.
The days grow shorter and the nights grow longer.
Every day in autumn is a fun day, nonetheless.

The air is cold and the leaves can't make sap,
The tree shuts down for a long winter nap.
And we will not see its leaves till springtime again.

Eimear Devlin (11)
Aquinas Diocesan Grammar School

A Boy's Dream

A boy's dream, football.
It was the night before my match,
My stomach was churning,
I had to play well.

Morning arrived and my nerves even worse,
We left for the stadium eagerly early,
My manager there in his Man Utd coat,
His short brown hair waved and curly.

The coach named the team,
Nolan no 7
My face turned white, my hands cold,
My voice croaking, my head buzzing.

We ran onto the pitch in our clean, new kit,
The clanking of the boots echoed through the tunnel
We started a warm-up, to get the blood pumping,
The ref blew his whistle to get the match started.

The match began at a frantic pace,
Tackles flying in, tension high,
Both teams looking for that little break,
Hearing the managers shouting, 'For goodness sake.'

The breakthrough came on the 20 minute mark
A diagonal ball was played through to the oncoming striker (me)
I took a touch, looked up and shot.

The ball flew like a rocket,
To the bottom corner of the net,
The crowd went wild, and I smiled
I was overcome with joy.

I ran to the crowd,
My teammates followed,
With an almighty pile on,
My manager bellowed,
'Get your mind on the game, you haven't finished.'

We ran to the pitch, our minds refocused,
We played on with a win in mind
Delighted when the final whistle blew,
Well, what can you say, a boy's dream came true.

Niall Nolan (13)
Aquinas Diocesan Grammar School

Performance

Suddenly I'm awake, a
Cold hand squeezing at my gut,
Fresh from hideous dreams
Where lines leave my mind
A small, empty room.

Backstage, alive with frantic
Chattering, we freeze to hear
The mumbling, burbling,
Grumbling murmur of the
Eager audience.

All eyes are focused on the
Huge, gaping mouth of the stage
As we strain to hear our cues.
In the wings we all cluster
Together in dread.

A surge of panic - My cue!
Blinking in the blinding glare
I swallow, tasting the sharp
Tang of fear, my mind vacant, void -
My prophecy true.

Then, like a prayer answered
My character comes coursing
Through my veins. I raise my head
Suddenly sure. I'm Belling
At the Coaching Inn.

Coirle Magee (12)
Aquinas Diocesan Grammar School

Charley

As we sat there huddled together in the closet,
So dark we could only make out shapes,
Charley was drawing nearer, bringing with him
The sound of wind and rain.

Our fear was getting bigger as we heard the windows shake.
Our supplies were getting smaller, the house was blowing away,
Oh please God, let me live to see another day.

Charley was getting bigger as the eye passed over our heads.
Oh I wish I was back in Belfast in the comfort of my bed.

The wind and rain were dying down as Charley drifted away.
Five hours he lingered over us, but no longer he would stay.

It was safe to leave, *thank God I'm in one piece,* I thought.
Then it was time to go out and see the damage that Charley had left
behind.

As I walked through the door,
The devastation around me was unbelievable.
The scattered debris, the floods and the fallen trees,
The broken glass, the missing roofs, the list goes on forever.

The power was out for three days and three nights
And the food was going off.
When it came back on we watched the TV news saying,
Frances is on the way!

Paul McCarney (12)
Aquinas Diocesan Grammar School

Rainy Day

Shall I compare thee to a rainy day?
Thou art more dull,
Thou art more grey,
But after a while the clouds will move,
The sun will emerge and make things good,
The sun is out, the clouds are away,
Now everyone can get on with their day!

Michael McCartney (15)
Aquinas Diocesan Grammar School

The Hospital Visit

I wasn't really scared in the car
Going to the hospital to see about my scar,
My mum seemed very jumpy, but organised
Like when she is nervous, so that's when I realised
That maybe this was serious.

It seemed like hours I was waiting for my turn
It got so hot it felt like I was going to burn.
Finally, at last came my name
But it was so quiet, it felt more like a walk of shame,
With everyone's glaring eyes on me.

When I sat down in the medical room;
The doctor was nice but his voice was an almighty boom.
He had looked at my arm and asked if I was in pain,
I told him it felt just the same.
He then went and had a discussion with the nurse.

The nurse came back and started getting things ready,
The instruments looked painful so I too started getting ready.
But it was all over in a minute so Mum and me left.
But on the way home,
Mum looked more terrified than going that morning.

Amy Salmon (13)
Aquinas Diocesan Grammar School

Busted!

Busted, I can't breathe without you,
If you weren't around, don't know what I'd do!
You can take me to the year 3000, I'd never say no!
You can take me anywhere you want to go.
I'm a raving Busted maniac you see
I'll be your Britney or Miss Mackenzie.
Busted, you rock and are the best band around,
'Cause you've got a unique and original sound.
Busted, you're number one,
So party on and have fun, fun, fun!

Amy Hamill (13)
Aquinas Diocesan Grammar School

Gone

It was hard to go on
But it was to be done
it was hard to look past what I knew was coming
They were leaving
I needed them to stay
It was hard to go on
But it was to be done.

These were the people who,
I lived to be
And they were leaving my life
I was beginning to see
I tried to block out
Imagine it wasn't true
That they weren't leaving me
These were the people who,
I lived to be
And they were leaving my life
I was beginning to see.

Then I looked and I saw
I see the person I am destined to be.
The person I need
and wanted with me
it wasn't their fault,
they told me at last
to stay here at home
like they had done in the past
I decided to leave
our time had passed
I was going
Was leaving for last.
Then I looked and I saw
I see the person I am destined to be.

I try hard not to forget
As each day has passed
It's all fading from my mind
and it's happening fast
but knowing some day
our paths will cross.

I'm finding leaving
Not so hard at last.

Aoife Monaghan (14)
Aquinas Diocesan Grammar School

Emergency!

Have to go to emergency room
Cos I hit my head on weights,
Waiting for ages in a creepy hospital
Is what my dad really hates.

Doctors came and went
But none were for my head,
Finally one showed us to
A small room with a bed.

He cleaned up my wound
And put in some stitches
And when he was done
He pulled up his breeches.

We left the Royal
And drove to our house,
Mum was glad I wasn't
Weak like a mouse.

When the stitches came out
The cut was a scar,
I was really happy
I felt like a star!

Shauna Leonard (14)
Aquinas Diocesan Grammar School

Changing Rooms

Waking up one morning,
Sale sign out front,
Puzzled at why
We might be moving house.

This dire old house,
My home for years,
Leaving it in the past,
Seemed so linear.

From my tiny room,
To the enormous house that awaits,
The change is a great deal.

Leaving behind those I know so well,
Memories pass,
Memories go,
Hold on to one tight,
Tight as a pillow.

All has passed,
Long and gone,
But when I look back,
Changing rooms wasn't such a bad idea.

Dominic Leeson (14)
Aquinas Diocesan Grammar School

The Sun

The sun, smiling warningly on the Earth
Eating the darkness in the morning
Throwing it back out at night
Eating the cold as a mother heats a child.

Waking people in the mornings
Smiling brightly in the sky
Rising high in the winter
Falling in the summer.

Matthew McParland (12)
Aquinas Diocesan Grammar School

Alone

I walk into a room full of strange faces,
I don't know what to say,
They don't know what it's like to be alone,
To be the new girl today.

The weeks went by slowly,
Nothing really changed.
They didn't get to know me,
To see the girl behind this face.

They thought I was happy,
How were they supposed to know?
I just wanted to be invisible,
To go where I could be alone.

Things never got any easier,
I started not to care.
I wanted to be alone,
The pain I could not bear.

So here I am, 13 now,
Happy with all my friends,
Only occasionally do I ever feel,
Alone once again.

Katherine McCann (13)
Aquinas Diocesan Grammar School

We Shall Meet Again

We shall meet again.
On that summer's day,
Down the dusty lane,
Past the barn full of hay.
The cows shall moo as you pass
And when you get to the gate
You shall hear the Sunday mass
And by fate
We shall meet again.

Madelaine Carey (14)
Aquinas Diocesan Grammar School

Holiday

My mum said, 'Time to get up at last!
Got to be outside the Opera House for half past.'
It's cold on Great Victoria Street
But we don't notice as we chat to strangers we meet.

By three the bus had taken us to the boat
I wanted to go outside, so I had to wear a coat.
Three hours later we arrived in Wales
We drove down the road to get some delicious meals.

We arrived at the hotel two hours before the match,
We all deserved a rest after a journey like that.
At 1 o'clock the match will start
So we get our reviews for Man U vs Stuttgart.

Inside the stadium, there were smiles all around
As both United's shots were goal bound.
The next day and we were home at last
To tell our friends of the excitement just past.

David Irvine (13)
Aquinas Diocesan Grammar School

Destination

What is fate? Does it even exist?
Are our lives planned out by a certain higher power
Or is our destiny decided with free will?

I can remember happy moments in my life, when I look back and
smile.
I look back at decisions and think of what it could have been,
Maybe happier for just a while.

But no matter what I do to try and control my fate,
Will I still end up at the same destination?
Is life just a journey which has a simple end
Or an adventure with many complicated roads to take?

Sarah Manning (14)
Aquinas Diocesan Grammar School

Rusty In The Morning

As I wake up in the morning
The sunlight blinds my eyes

When I'm woken in the morning
My dad's singing hurts my ears

I feel like giving him a slap
I crawl out of bed and suffer the weight of the world on my back.

My eyes so crusty
My joints feel so old and rusty.

Hot butter spread over my breakfast toast
This is the only thing I like, I love it the most.

School and evil teachers aren't so far away
It's the same thing I fear, over and over every day.

Nobody likes the morning,
it's so cold, dull and boring.

Darren Quigley (12)
Aquinas Diocesan Grammar School

The Sun

Smiling down,
Beating on my face,
It follows me around,
Filled with grace!

Until it hides behind a cloud,
Then I feel a little sad,
But when it peeks out again,
I start to feel a little glad!

Without the sun,
It would be dull and grey,
I wouldn't enjoy it,
Because the sun makes my day!

Marion McGuigan (13)
Aquinas Diocesan Grammar School

Ice Skating Or Swimming

I had a choice to make,
I didn't know which one to take,
It was like a gate, which one to open,
Which one to take?

To go to a swimming pool
That would be cool
To go skating on ice
That would be nice.

I had a choice to make,
I didn't know which one to take,
Either swimming with my brother, Mum and Dad,
Or ice-skating to my cousin's party, that would be mad.

I decided to go to the ice rink,
I felt like I was going to sink
It was my first time
It was all fine, until . . .

I was skating along, everything was nice,
Next second I was down on the ice
Someone skated over my finger, it was covered
In blood, the red ice was like a flood.

I was brought to a hospital bed,
I wished I had gone swimming instead.

Lisa Gilmore (13)
Aquinas Diocesan Grammar School

The Wait

Sitting in a waiting room,
Waiting, waiting, waiting for doom.
The clock says an hour, though it feels like a day,
Outside the trees swish and sway.
I hear a cry, more time goes by.

They soon arrive, their will to strive.
Our party expands, us three hold hands.
Two hours now, but I don't see how,
How long have we been sitting here
Waiting, waiting, waiting in fear?
Why are we waiting, stupidly debating?
They aren't looking, now's your chance.

I make a run, like a bullet from a gun.
I stop and see him there
Crying, it's hard to bear.
This doesn't make sense, I don't understand,
Why is he crying, holding his hand?
A distant shout for me to come back
Back to waiting.

Sitting in a waiting room,
Outside the world looks dark and gloom.
Inside's the same, they're all to blame.
Three hours have passed, the memory will last.
He died early morn, just as she was born.

Orla Crawford (13)
Aquinas Diocesan Grammar School

Can Friendship Ever Last?

Making my way up to school,
I wondered if I would be a reject or cool,
I saw a girl as scared as I
And went up to her just to say hi.

Two years have passed since that day
And things have changed in a dramatic way.
I trusted her with my biggest worry in life
And in my back, she stuck a knife.
I told her not to tell a soul,
But for some attention
She told lots of boys in the school,
So that I would look the biggest fool.
She just kept going, telling my secrets and lying,
Until I gave up and started crying.
That was last May and I still haven't spoken to her from that day.

I have other friends that I can trust,
But I only tell them things if I must.
Have I moved on?
If I had, I don't think I would be writing this poem.
Life goes so fast,
But can friendship ever last?

Joanna Quigg (13)
Aquinas Diocesan Grammar School

The Sun

The sun beams down on us,
Like a glowing face.
Each morning it greets us
With its warm embrace.
And at night it goes,
Out come the winking stars
Until it comes again
In the early hours.

Claire Gunn (13)
Aquinas Diocesan Grammar School

My Granda

In hospital I remember visiting him,
I remember walking down the long hall
I remember it had a strange smell and the lights were very dim!

I remember walking into the room
And he was lying on his bed,
He was fast asleep
With a book over his head.

I remember the nurse saying
He would be out in one more day,
He would eventually go home
And my granny was soon on the phone.

After he was a few days at home
He wanted to put on his best suit,
He lifted a picture of our family
And on the table beside his bed was where it was put.

The next day he never woke up
It was soon after that that my mum phoned us,
We were so worried
We went down there in a rush.

I remember how empty I felt
I just sat there staring,
I felt no emotion
My dad was so caring.

When we finally arrived at my granny's house
Everyone was so nice,
I went to say goodbye to him
To the touch, he was as cold as ice.

So I would just like to say
That every time I pray,
I say,
Granda I miss you
And I will hopefully see you again some day!

Katie McGrath (14)
Aquinas Diocesan Grammar School

The Crash

I called home
My mum wasn't there,
My brother sounded sad
So my auntie came to me.
When I got into the car
I knew there was something wrong,
I just knew it
My brother Ronan was in hospital
He was hit by a car
And had a blood clot on his brain.

I couldn't see him
Mum said it was scary,
My dad was in America
And had to leave.
Ronan had a breathing machine
But he couldn't speak
He didn't understand
And got very annoyed, like me.

All the teachers got to see him
But I wasn't allowed.
I got very upset
And didn't understand,
But why?

Once he could breathe,
I went to see him.
But when I had to go home,
I wanted to stay with him forever.
Stay with him forever.

Since that day,
We've all gotten closer.
Especially Ronan and I.
He is back to himself
And having a great time,
We've all gotten closer
Especially Ronan and I . . .

Olivia McKillop (13)
Aquinas Diocesan Grammar School

Dreams Really Do Come True

It's 6.30am
I know what you are thinking
And the answer is yes.
There is a world before 10 on the holidays.
I have to get my gear on and my contacts in
So that I am ready to get skating at 8.

As we set out for Dundonald
Something was very different.
The roads were as empty as a biscuit tin in our house.
The only thing that stirred
Was a bird singing its morning tune.
It was as if time had stood still
No cars, no red lights, nothing.

It's now around 7.30
And it's time to get signed in.
My free bottle of Powerade in one hand
Stick in the other.
As we stepped onto the glossy ice,
Our skates tore into it like
The sound of something scraping glass.

The two long, hard hours were over
And the off ice fun began.
Two hours of baseball,
Football and hockey tactics
Eat into the day.
Day 1 was over
Let Day 2 begin.

As the week went on
All 50 of us got into a
Regular routine.
The smells of the Zamboni fumes
As we walked through the doors to the rigorous training.
The feeling of success that I had fulfilled my dream
To train with the Giants.

Richard Gault (13)
Aquinas Diocesan Grammar School

The Local Derby

Today was the day of the Derby,
I had butterflies in my stomach.
As I sat in the changing rooms shivering,
The tension and atmosphere building.

As we made our way to the pitch,
Our boots clashed against the hard concrete.
When the ref blew his whistle,
It made a deafening screech,
All through the ground like a high-pitched scream.

The match was close, but in the end we won,
Our hard work and training had been worth it.
When I think back to that great victory
And the really high score,
I don't think we could have done any more.

Sean Irwin (14)
Aquinas Diocesan Grammar School

The School Walk

The school walk never really looked forward to.
The hurried, near run in the freezing cold winter morning.
Then a moment of relief while leaping onto the bus
With the tingling sensation of going from cold to hot quickly.
The fee is paid but the worry doesn't end there.
No, there is still the worry of,
'Have you got everything you need for school?'
Is some important item left forlorn in the warm hall with the
                                                smell of toast?
Is the bus going to be on time?
Still, all you can do is eager the bus along . . .
When you arrive at your destination,
You just have to get through the day and look forward to the next.

Barry Curran (12)
Aquinas Diocesan Grammar School

A New Life

The first thing I remember,
About that day,
Is being in Karen's car going to the airport,
Looking back at the disappearing figure of my dad.
I had such a feeling that it hurt.

I sound like I regret
The decision made for me.
For if I stayed there,
How unhappy I would be.

I knew this day was coming,
For a couple of months.
But didn't know why,
Why we had to fly.

I sound like I regret,
The decision made for me,
For if I stayed there,
How unhappy I would be.

David Poole (13)
Aquinas Diocesan Grammar School

Ocean

Shall I compare thee to the ocean?
Like the changing of the tide,
Rough winds do shake the earth and sea,
Then all becomes gentle and oh so peaceful,
The sun shines upon it and the world's beauty is reflected,
Underneath its glassy shield is a hidden world,
So beautiful that all eyes should see.
It shall never fade nor disappear,
Time will not take it, as it is carved into the earth,
Like a piece of history being carved into a stone,
Many a person has been taken by the monster it is,
Never to return again, at the bottom of the ocean they shall remain.

Christine McIlvenny (16)
Aquinas Diocesan Grammar School

Underwater Holiday

I went to Spain
It was great, I was only young
I went with mates
It was really fun.
We almost missed the plane
So we had to run.

We got there, I was excited
To get into the pool
I ran and ran across the warm ground
It felt great to be in the sun.

When we were over there
It was my sister's birthday
I couldn't wait for the pool again
I sat beside the pool on my bum
I nearly drowned
Thanks to my mum I'm still alive!

Holidays are great
I can't wait
For my next one!

Mark Dornan (13)
Ashfield Boys' High School

Football Life

The best parts of a football match
Are when you are getting changed
In the lovely warm changing room
And splashing on the winter green.

After that, coming down the tunnel with shivers up your back
And hearing the crowd roar coming onto the wet and cold pitch
Then staying on your toes, keeping yourself warm
Waiting for the whistle
Before you start your excitement.

And that's the best part of a football match.

Wayne Drummond (12)
Ashfield Boys' High School

Hallowe'en

The night is dark, the night is cold
The children dress in days of old.
Witches, wizards, goblins and ghouls
They run around the street like fools
Collecting money, that's their loot.

They do not want you to know their name
They want you to play along with their game
Of bubbling cauldrons and Hallowe'en tales
Of witches, mice and slimy snails.

So if they knock upon your door
Don't shoot at them, don't rant, don't roar.
The only monsters they should see
Are the Hallowe'en ones on TV.

Put some silver in their pot
It will make them happy, and that's the lot.

Jamie Shaw (13)
Ashfield Boys' High School

Saturday Fishing

This Saturday I went fishing
It was raining heavily
It was freezing cold
My feet were like blocks of ice
So the man who owned the lake
Invited us in for tea
There were waves like at sea
So we decided to go to the far end of the lake to fish
It was great
It was fun
It was exciting
Seven trout in the bag for me
And eight for my friend, for his family for tea.

Nathan Gilbert (13)
Ashfield Boys' High School

A Winter's Morning

First thing in the morning I get out of bed,
Go downstairs and butter my bread.
Pour some cereal, but have no milk
Standing in my pyjamas made of silk.

Go into the living room, turn on TV
First channel on is the BBC.
Sit down in the chair and put my feet up
Getting cold, so I turn the heat up.

Go upstairs to get into my clothes
Grab a handkerchief to blow my nose.
Open the door to see that it's white
Snow on the hills, oh what a sight.

I am going to the shop, just down the street
The snow is crunching at my feet.
Go into the shop and get some Fanta
Man on the corner dressed as Santa.

Walking down the street, happy as can be
A robin redbreast is sitting in the tree.
It is cold, people are moaning
It's just a typical winter's morning.

Alan Graham (14)
Ashfield Boys' High School

David

D oesn't like French
A lways late
V ery funny
I s never working
D oesn't do homework.

David Beattie (13)
Ashfield Boys' High School

One Cold Saturday Morning

Balls flying left, right and centre
The midfielders don't know where to venture.
The goalkeeper's so bored while washing his vapours
He doesn't know whether to read his newspapers
One cold Saturday morning.

Strikers shooting from every angle
Defenders getting caught in a mangle
Midfielders filled with passion
Strikers finishing in a style of fashion
One cold Saturday morning.

While defenders play with pride
Midfielders making that final slide
Superstars made every day
While the grass slowly turns to hay
One cold Saturday morning.

Football is a rough game
Just like making a lion tame
Children watching and crying
While the ball is flying
One cold Saturday morning.

Neil Allen (14)
Ashfield Boys' High School

Birds

B eautiful and colourful, they bring life to places
I nteresting species each with different faces
R obins, cuckoos, nightingales, each species with a different call
D eafening if you are standing in a field full of geese
S parrows, swans and starlings, I love to watch them all.

Jonathan Beckett (13)
Ashfield Boys' High School

Eating And Sleeping

When I'm sleeping in the night
Then the birds come out to play
And I get a sudden fright.
When they start to sing early in
The morning.

In the morning when I eat my breakfast
I go to the toilet
A robin eats my bacon and egg
When I go and sit down
It takes my bacon and some toast.

Henry Milne (12)
Ashfield Boys' High School

Anger

Anger is in us no matter what
And whatever we do we cannot make it stop
It comes out in different ways
Shouting, swearing and fighting
But in a way you can control it
It just depends on what you do
But if you don't control it
It will eat and tear away at you.

Ryan Miskelly (14)
Ashfield Boys' High School

Cola

The only tasty drink
Mmm as it glistens in the sun
Shining brown liquid in a glass
It fizzes and bubbles when it enters your mouth
And touches your tongue
It makes you fizz with excitement for more.

Kriss Brown (13)
Ashfield Boys' High School

What A Swing!

There I was in my moment
I was in a golf tournament
It was my turn to do the putting
Almost everyone was tutting.
When I missed the hole
I tried not to cry
When it was a tie
I felt I could die
I had another chance to hit it in
And I started to dance
That's when I hit it in
And the other guy missed
I won the trophy
And it weighed a ton
I'm so glad
It was me that won!

Wade Aitken (13)
Ashfield Boys' High School

Friends

I never wanted this day to come
When we would have to part
Because our friendship means
So much to me.

I secretly break my heart
Off to our separate homes we go
Remembering all the good times
The lovely days we spent together.

It's always on my mind
I hope the day very soon will come
When we will meet again
Because my friend, you mean a lot to me.

Samuel Crothers (13)
Ashfield Boys' High School

Another Monday

Today I got up on the wrong side of bed
I got in the car
I felt like I'm dead
Stiff, tired and I've got a sore head.

Getting past the traffic,
It's just a waste
It's like trying to win a Formula 1 race.

I get to school
Feel a bit more alive
But it's a Monday at school
I wonder if I'll survive.

Lunchtime's here
I jump up with glee,
But after lunch
I've got a teacher to see.

Another Monday's over now
It went quite fast,
I don't know how
But I've managed to last.

David Wilton (13)
Ashfield Boys' High School

Food So Simple

My food is simple and easy to cook
All my friends come to have a look
It's so simple, it hardly takes any time
Just put it in the microwave for a little while
My friends they love it, they come back for more
Shall I tell you its name?
It's spaghetti for four!

Lee Carson (14)
Ashfield Boys' High School

My Pet

I have a pet named George
He's an old and lazy cat.
All he does is sit there
And gets fat.

One day I saw him try to move
So I helped him cross the room
All he did was sit there
Purring in the gloom.

I saw him trying to eat slowly
One bit of food at a time
He only had about four
Then he dropped dead on the floor.

The moral of the tale
Is if you have a cat
Make sure it gets regular exercise
Don't feed it till it's fat.

Ross McGivern (13)
Ashfield Boys' High School

The War

The war was many years ago
It lasted about two years or so
There were many fighters
But the number of men got tighter and tighter.

There were bombs all over the place
Which hit some soldiers in the face
Guns were fired from all around
And everybody was hiding underground.

The war was all over
And the last man fell over
The last soldiers cheered
And went off to celebrate to have a drink of beer.

Laurie Caruth (14)
Ashfield Boys' High School

Balance

Where one world ends another begins.
Where one man regrets another man sins.
Where one man is healed another is hurt.
While one man rests another must work.
When one life arrives another must go.
When one great tree falls another must grow.
When one man is starving another is fed.
Where one man is homeless another's in bed.
We must make the goods more and make the bads less,
So few men are cursed and most men are blessed.
We must undo the wrongs and increase the rights
And wherever there is darkness we'll renew with light.
We must reject the evil and embrace the good,
Grant the sinners forgiveness and the starving with food.
But for some years to come these hopes remain dreams,
For when one man is silent another man screams.

Ben Dinnen (14)
Ashfield Boys' High School

Foods I Like

Chips are the best,
they are warm, chewy and filling,
but they are fattening so don't eat too much,
but I think chicken nuggets are nicer.

Chicken nuggets are gorgeous,
they are delicious, but hot,
they are hard, crunchy, lovely and chewy,
but jelly is much nicer.

Jelly is much better,
it is mostly cold, wobbly, gooey and smooth,
but it is so lovely you can't stop eating it.

Robert Black (12)
Ashfield Boys' High School

Christmas

All things shine at Christmas time
Christmas is a happy time
Presents bunched up in the corner
How exciting! I can't wait!
Christmas poppers make a *bang!*
Bright things hang from the tree,
Snow outside, that's all I see.

All things shine at Christmas time,
Everyone has a happy time
A snowball fight you just might
Get a Christmas treat
Walking in the snow
With your feet so cold
The multicoloured trees
They all look so old.

Steven McLean (12)
Ashfield Boys' High School

Football Guide

Football is a brilliant sport
Played by people tall and small
The goalkeeper is at the back
Stopping the ball from going past.
The defenders are there, to help him through
Making sure to hit the ball.
The midfielders are in the middle as the name suggests
They are there to pass the ball
So the attackers can hit it into the back of the net
The crowds will cheer in sheer delight
As their team scores a goal.

Tafozzul Haque (12)
Ashfield Boys' High School

The Horror Of War

The horrors of war
Are hard to believe
The drone of the planes
And the tremble of the bombs.

Inside the shelter
All is quiet
Everything is black
No light, no sounds.

For an hour or two
Everything is quiet
Waiting for the 'all clear'
Eventually it comes.

Outside rubble everywhere
Wondering if our house is OK
Walking round the streets, all is demolished
Just waiting to see if our house is OK.

Mark Higgins (14)
Ashfield Boys' High School

Scared

I can't sleep and it's getting late
I hear the howling of wolves
I think about ghosts and ghouls
I see shadows on the wall.
I hear creaking floorboards in the hall
I am sweating
I hear weird noises everywhere
I start to think of monsters underneath my bed
Cutting off my head
Then the most scary thought hits me
I forgot to do my homework.

Rory Coalter (12)
Ashfield Boys' High School

A Sport Report

To swim a mile,
Requires some style.

It takes some pace,
To win a race.

When surfing a wave,
You must be brave.

It would be supreme,
To flip on the beam.

To sink the pink,
You need to think.

It's quite the trend,
To parascend.

If you're three under par,
You will go far.

To hit the wicket,
Is great in cricket.

All of these sports are good to do,
So get up and find the best one for you!

Philip McBride (12)
Ashfield Boys' High School

Snowy Days

Snowy days are bliss
As our daily school we miss
All day long out in the snow
Pelting all my mates as I go
Freezing fingers, freezing toes
My face has got a rosy glow
Hoping and praying that tomorrow
There's lots more snow and no sorrow
Otherwise it's back to school and stuff
And our English teacher Mr Duff.

Jack Moore (14)
Ashfield Boys' High School

The Black Man

In that old haunted house
You can hear footsteps, mostly a mouse.
In the shadow was a man
Then I heard the kicking of a can.

The smell in there is like sawdust
On the table was a bread crust.
Beside the table was a coffin
Then I heard somebody coughing.

When I went around the back
I nearly tiptoed over a sack.
That very big garden was a graveyard,
Not even one single greeting card.

When I tiptoed up the stairs
I felt a breeze and got the scares.
I looked around for an open window
All I found was a man with a crow.

He tried to choke me with his hand
Then I hit him with an elastic band.
I ran downstairs and out the door
Then it began to pour and pour.

David McLearnon (13)
Ashfield Boys' High School

My Football Poem

On Saturday morning subs are being made.
Slide tackles are flying in and goals are getting scored.
And sometimes you get bored
But when a goal is scored, you are not bored.
Players get hurt, managers panic, medics run on
Player comes off, sub goes on.
He should have got a yellow card, but the referees are never fair
Especially the ones with no hair.
But we don't care, because we are winning the tie
And we will support, until we die.

Curtis Howe (12)
Ashfield Boys' High School

War

War is terrible
Fighting and killing
Bombs and guns
Waiting to die
In the trenches cold and wet
You can't make friends here
Because they will all die
Because Hitler wanted to take over
But we said *no!*
So this is how it is started
I wish it could all go away
And the Germans you can keep them at bay!
I want to go home to see my wife
But I will fight for my country
Day and night,
Then we hear the celebrations in 1945
I'm glad I'm still alive
I've been in the war for five years now
I shouted and screamed!
The war is over!
I can now go home and live my life
I can't believe it
I have survived the war.

Jonathan Thompson (12)
Ashfield Boys' High School

Chinese

When I get a Chinese
My excitement builds.
I can smell my dinner coming
And bubbling all the way from my room.
I run downstairs
And look at the curry in front of me
Then I get stuck in.

Aaron Clarke (11)
Ashfield Boys' High School

Snowball Fight

Splosh, that hit me in the face,
Whack, and in my belly!
Fizz, that took my woolly hat
And dripped into my wellies!

Whoosh, hee, hee, I got him back,
Oops! But that one's missed!
Now they're coming thick and fast,
Snowy balls as big as fists!

It must be time to call a truce,
Before I'm soaked right through!
My brother's just too good at this
And my hands are turning blue!

But snowball fights are such good fun,
Even though it's cold and wet!
So just one more and here it goes,
Splat! I got him on his neck!

Christopher Blacker (12)
Ashfield Boys' High School

Injury Time

A cold winter's day, the team are about to play.
First tackle, muddy face, aches and pains today.
'It's a scrum,' the ref is about to say.
A kick to the face.
The boy faces down on the ground.
He gets back to play another kick to start the game.
Our striped jerseys covered in blood or mud.
The other team on the run, to get their first try.
Our back sends him down.
But this time the boy is about to say,
'I can't get up today!'

Jackson Hutchinson (12)
Ashfield Boys' High School

Hallowe'en

On Hallowe'en night,
You're sure of a fright,
When the spooks come out to play,
They wail and scream if you know what I mean,
Oh what an eerie sight.

To make a monster spell
Stir it up and mix it well,
Add eye of lizard,
Toe of frog,
Tail of rat
And bark of dog.

To make a monster spell
Stir it up and mix it well,
Web of spider,
Slime of toad,
Squish of hedgehog,
Scraped from a road.

Now it's done,
The spell is ready,
The monster's rising,
Slow and steady.

But the time is ready for the sun to rise
And the spooks all vanish before your eyes,
They've had great fun on Hallowe'en night,
Will you see them next year? Well you just might . . .

Stephen Rooney (14)
Ashfield Boys' High School

Ashfield Boys' Rap

So I'm here in Ashfield,
Ashfield Boys' High School
And I tell you this school is not for fools.
So we've got English first
And Mrs Pryce comes up with her purse
And says 'Kids go to my car
And drive away far
Because we have a spelling exam'
So two minutes later her car is crammed.
Now we're in French with Mrs Porter,
She asks so many questions like a news reporter.
So we're back in history with Mrs Pryce
Telling us all about King Henry's wives.
So now we're at PE with Mr Spence,
And I say to him 'No offence
But can we play soccer instead of cricket
Because I keep getting hit with the bloody wicket.'
So now it's home time
But before I go
If you're coming out later
Give me a phone!

Dale Lockhart (13)
Ashfield Boys' High School

Grounded

Getting grounded is the worst thing that can happen,
No fun, no mates and especially no laughing.
You say to yourself, 'I wish I hadn't have done what I did.'
If I was grounded for a million years, I couldn't live.
You're grounded because you did something wrong
Or you're bad news to school,
Half the time you're grounded you feel as if your mum is glued to you,
Being grounded is something I just can't be living with,
You beg and you beg, but you know that Mum ain't giving in.

Raymond Algie (14)
Ashfield Boys' High School

I'm A Teacher's Pet

I kicked the teacher
I bet she thought I couldn't reach her,
Then I kicked her with my heel
So she let out a squeal.

I picked up a handful of sand
Then it sort of slipped out of my hand
It hit someone in the eyes
So I put on a disguise.

As I crawled along the ground
Trying not to make a sound
But all of a sudden the teacher sat me on a chair.
I was having so much fun and she ruined it, so I got angry so I
pulled her hair.

My mum came and collected me
And shouted at me from 1 o'clock till half-past three,
And when I got home
I got a slap on the dome.

Christopher Kemp (13)
Ashfield Boys' High School

Football Mad

I like football, watching it on television or playing it with my mates!
I like doing nets so much so that I have broken my wrist saving a goal!
My favourite football team is Glasgow Rangers Football Club.
Their stadium is called Ibrox Park.
The team mascot is Broxi Bear.
Their goalkeeper is called Stefan Klos and he is class!
It is a standing joke in my family that I am always playing football,
So much so that I have five footballs!
It was my birthday yesterday and can you guess what I got?
Yes, a football, new goalkeeper's gloves,
New football boots and the Northern Ireland goalkeeper's kit.
I just love football!

Jordyn Ralston (12)
Ashfield Boys' High School

The Rescued Dog

As I watch you running through the sea,
Strong and sleek with endless energy.
I think of what your life might be,
Had you not come to live with me.

Locked up in a cupboard cold and dark,
Too afraid to move, fight back or bark,
They wanted to make you a fighting machine,
To break your spirit and make you mean.

All those men broke down the door
Brought you out and set you free,
You were taken to a brief new 'home'
With the hope of a new family.

Now standing tall so big and strong
All those bad memories hopefully gone,
No longer scared or all alone
Now you stand proud in your loving home.

Adam Shanley (13)
Ashfield Boys' High School

Pressures

Pressures in all our work
And in everything we do
Pressures in our blood
And pouring over you
But still we try and live with it
We try and kill the pain
Like living in a wooden house
That slowly burns in vain
But the pressure always gets to us
And starts to eat away
Until the pressure gets too much
And then we fade away.

Matthew Hamilton (14)
Ashfield Boys' High School

Hallowe'en

Hallowe'en is so much fun
Lighting fireworks when there is no sun,
Kids running about the street,
Wrapping your door and saying trick or treat.

The firework goes up into the cloud
It explodes and is really loud,
When the colours fill the sky
You see a rocket flying by.

People try to frighten you
They jump out and say boo!
Kids dress up in scary stuff
But not as scary as Mr Duff.

Kids get a lot to eat
By going to doors and saying trick or treat,
Some people give them fruit to eat
Others give them sweets as a treat.

All the children put on false faces
To scare people from different places
And that's all I've got to say
About this Hallowe'en day.

Johnathon Pavis (13)
Ashfield Boys' High School

Scary Poem

Goblins and warlocks,
Ghosts and ghouls
Waiting outside the mortals' schools.
As they walk or take-off by flight
They are sure to give you a giant fright!
As you wake up to tie your shoes
They are out there climbing on statues.
So next time you turn the corner to go to school
You might just turn it and hear a loud, *boo!*

John Williams (12)
Ashfield Boys' High School

Just An Ordinary Day

A few friends, a football
A beautiful day
Sun streaming down
Warm sun's rays caressing us
Everything was good
Happiness
Birdsong in the background
A goal
Everyone smiling
A day of recorded time
Then suddenly . . .
News came
It was David
He'd been taken to hospital
Suddenly the ray changed.
A cloud levelled out the sun
We looked at each other in silence
Until we heard the update
Our cousin would survive.
Suddenly the sun came out again
And we went out into the hot rays
To rid us of our cold.

David Nesbitt (15)
Ashfield Boys' High School

Hallowe'en

H aunted houses, bats and rats
A fter midnight there is no light
L ots of scary costumes, are they real?
L unch could be you!
O h no, run away, don't come for your share
W itches, goblins, ghouls are here.
E ver so scary sounds and faces
E ven the weather starts to change
N ow it's morning, what happened again?

Ryan McCoy (12)
Ashfield Boys' High School

The Feeling Of A Coin

My body shook with fear,
My heart skipped a beat,
There was no one there.
A coin fell out of my pocket
And rolled around the ground,
It disappeared down the grating,
Which was rather irritating.
'Go back home,'
A little voice said.
But I can't,
Not as things stand.
My mum and dad's rowing,
Is way out of hand
And so I stay alone,
In these hostile streets,
I turn up to see who's out there,
Jumping suddenly
Otherwise being scared,
Like a child alone
Among enormous toys.

Christopher Nelson (16)
Ashfield Boys' High School

Hallowe'en

H owls of ghosts and cries from banshees
A nd heaps of sweet, sweet candy
L ots of fun and games
L oads of people run, run, run
O ut with the darkness
W itches fly in the
E mpty, darkened sky
E very hour that goes by
N ot too scared, but very shy the children have heaps more fun.

Nicky Telford (12)
Ashfield Boys' High School

Hallowe'en

Ghouls and ghosts,
Goblins and graveyards,
Witches and warlocks,
Scary faces,
Dark places.
See the darkness in their eyes,
Pumpkins and costumes
Lantern's light
You're in for a fright.
Beware, there is something in the air!
Werewolves howling,
Banshees squealing
As the children trick or treat something lurks
Beneath their feet,
As it is Hallowe'en
night!

Chris Tollerton (12)
Ashfield Boys' High School

Choppers

The wind in your face
Wheels turning fast,
The piston's pumping,
A loud groaning noise from the engine
Like it's shouting out at me.

Straight long road ahead
Cows and sheep in the field,
The fresh smell of the countryside.
The feel of the grips as I change gear
The sun burning my neck.

Bears, moose other wildlife on the edge of the road
No cars in 20 to 30 miles
As I stop at the edge of the road
I watch the sun go down.

Adam Dickinson (13)
Ashfield Boys' High School

My Family At Christmas Time

Wake up, wake up, Christmas is here
It's time for everyone to share the Christmas cheer.

Laughter, giggling, mouth-watering food
Mother, father, sister saying boo
Auntie, uncle, having a chuckle
Granny, granda, resting their knuckles

Dinner, here it comes
I can't wait, yum, yum, yum
Dishes, dishes, not for me
I think I will hide behind the Christmas tree

Presents, presents, everywhere
And loads and loads to share

All the family sing Christmas cheer
Then my dad brings out the Christmas beer
The children play with their toys
With all the girls and boys

It's dark, it's late, Christmas Day is gone
Roll on Boxing Day, it won't be long.

Kingsley Davidson (12)
Ashfield Boys' High School

Cauliflower Cheese

The creamy sauce surrounding the
Big coal-like vegetable all yellow.
The melt of it on your tongue,
The smell of it reflecting on a
Big Mac meal and large chips.
The sensational feeling that I
Get when I see it, it reminds
Me of a Mars bar slowly going
Down my throat.

Ben Uprichard (12)
Ashfield Boys' High School

The Foot

The foot is big and has a bunion,
It makes you cry like an onion,
The horrible foot is missing a toe,
He never washes them so they smell of BO.

The whole foot looks so bad,
Five little toes it once had,
The foot, the smell, it looks like fog,
That whole foot smells like a bog.

The heel is like a crunchy biscuit,
Chop it off, lose it, or risk it,
Losing your foot would be a terrible thing,
Your foot is a smelly ming.

In-between your toes are green,
Your baby toe looks like a bean,
Under your toenails are purple-red,
Your diseased foot is almost dead.

The end is near,
In fact it's here,
Sorry to say I have to shoot,
Your full on crazy, messed up foot!

Curtis Spence (14)
Ashfield Boys' High School

Bully

He follows me about everywhere I go.
He pushes me about when I'm at school.
He knows I fear him, there's nothing I can do
There is no one to talk to.
I cannot think, there's nothing I haven't tried.
But I pull myself together, so I don't cry.
Someone stands up for me, I didn't tell him to.
Now that boy's left this school
I'm free to go, well I think so!

Geoffrey Atkinson (12)
Ashfield Boys' High School

War

Bombs and bullets flying all around,
Friends and kin dying on the ground.
All kinds of aeroplanes taking flight,
Looking up from the ground, it's a terrible sight!

Ships and submarines, tanks and guns,
Taking away fathers, brothers and sons.
Mothers, sisters and daughters will pray,
Hoping their kin will come back some day.

Now in Flanders field the poppies do grow,
But back then the blood of soldiers did flow.
Was it for power? Was it for glory?
Myself thinking back it was a sad story.

On the eleventh hour, of the eleventh day,
Of the eleventh month
We will remember them when we pray.

Stephen Magill (12)
Ashfield Boys' High School

War Poem

On Monday night it began
I heard the first shot of a gun.
I grabbed my stuff and something to eat
And down to the shelter in my bare feet.
I heard an engine chuck chuck
And a big shout saying, 'Duck! Duck!'
The first bang was very loud,
It could have deafened a big crowd.
The second bang was not too bad
Inside now I was feeling bad.
The stay in the shelter was very long
I could smell something wrong.
When I got out I saw my pet mouse
And looked up quickly, where's my house?

Jonathan Sheil (14)
Ashfield Boys' High School

Ghouls And Ghosts

H appy and scary times
A dventurous without doubt
L ook out there are witches about
L aughing at fear
O pening your bag to see what's inside
W hile you look at your candy, you spot at the tip of your eye,
    a vampire just swinging on by
E choing through the air, screams of horror, bats are chirping,
    I think I know, is it because Dracula is dropping by?
E arwigs you see, and all of a sudden warlocks sap them on by
N ever knowing when this nightmare will end.

Ross McMillan (12)
Ashfield Boys' High School

Hallowe'en

H allowe'en is here, people die of fright,
A fter midnight strikes look who's here.
L aughter and joy, until Count Dracula is here,
L oving fireworks, but one shot down a witch!
O nly the next day are we able to play.
W e scare the neighbours but Frankenstein scares us!
E very Hallowe'en it's not safe,
E very night you think it's safe,
N ever go out again!

Jonathan Dalzell (11)
Ashfield Boys' High School

Golf Poem

G olf is great,
O nly on summer days,
L ong days playing,
F orget my troubles are there.

Christopher Walker (13)
Ashfield Boys' High School

Hallowe'en

H allowe'en is near
A t Hallowe'en night I will fear.
L ate at night witches come out.
L ads come out and give a shout.
O h, here it comes, 'Trick or treat?'
W ould I give them a sweet?
E vening is here
E ven the children are having dreams.
N ot the ghouls!

Ryan Hill (11)
Ashfield Boys' High School

Christmas

C hristmas is the best time of year.
H appiness all through Christmas.
R eally nice dinner on Christmas Day.
 I n Christmas you give and receive presents.
S elections of the best chocolate for Christmas.
T insel everywhere.
M asses of decorations everywhere.
A tree with twinkling lights all over,
S parkling from every direction.

Michael McMillan (11)
Ashfield Boys' High School

Burger

B eautiful bites of Burger King meat,
U nder the bap there's lots to eat.
R adish in some or radish in none.
G orgeous burgers and chips as well.
E ating the burgers makes you want more and more.
R otten or not it's nice to me.

Stephen Hamilton (11)
Ashfield Boys' High School

The Birds Of Doom

The birds of doom fly overhead
Ready to drop their load of doom
You can hear the chug chug
Of their engines.

They can't hear the cries
From below
They can't see the damage
They caused below.

They leave as they came
To get a new load of doom
To come back tomorrow
To cause mayhem.

Laurence Boyle (14)
Ashfield Boys' High School

Spicy Pastie

S picy but good
P lus it's brilliant food
I t rumbles in my belly
C urry is so smelly
Y is it so good? It's brilliant food.

P asties are as nice
A s curry and rice
S alt and pepper
T ogether are crackers
I like all foods
E ating in all different moods.

Jamie Edgar (12)
Ashfield Boys' High School

Irresistible Food

Irresistible food
I could dream about food
I could eat it all day
It's a beam from Heaven
I love chicken curry
Prawn crackers and a drink too
Because of the hot curry
It's like eating a hot ball of fire
It's good.

Curtis Adams (12)
Ashfield Boys' High School

My Mum

Friends will come and they will go,
For days, for months, for years.
But one friend is very special to me,
She will be there till the end.
No matter what I do or say
Good or bad or mean
I hold a special place for her,
My mum, it's her I need.

Adam Suitor (14)
Ashfield Boys' High School

Coco Pops, Coco Pops

Coco Pops, Coco Pops
Crispy and crunchy.
Coco Pops, Coco Pops
Sugary and sweet.
Coco Pops, Coco Pops
Snap, crackle and pop.
Coco Pops, Coco Pops,
Yummy in my tummy.

David Tipping (12)
Ashfield Boys' High School

Transylvania

Transylvania is a cursed place,
It is full of vampires, werewolves and Frankenstein's monster,
You can hear their victims' screams night after night,
As they devour them with delight.

He has no heart, so he feels nothing,
He cannot be killed by mortal means,
He has no reflection in any mirror,
He is Dracula lord of vampires.

If bitten by them you become one,
Men by day, but when the moon is full they turn into monsters,
They roam the streets looking for victims,
They are werewolves, the children of the night.

What was dead is now alive,
Several parts of several men were put together to make one,
A giant of a man, eight foot in height,
Created by a scientist and grave robber,
It is Frankenstein's monster.

Transylvania is a cursed place,
A place without a soul,
It's a place without a human face,
Where evil is the goal.

Neil Butler (13)
Ashfield Boys' High School

My Brother And Me

My brother and me, we never agree
Especially when it's time for tea,
He'll rush down the stairs
Knock into the chairs, to be first to be fed
Mum's hands on her head
This is the time of the day that she dreads.

Rian Budde (11)
Ashfield Boys' High School

Christmas

Christmas, Christmas
Plenty to do,
Mum's running round,
In a stew.

Cards to be written
Presents to wrap,
Needless to say
Dad's not in a flap.

Bath to be taken
New pyjamas put on,
Stocking hung up
Hopefully up at dawn.

Christmas morning
Here at last,
Last night went in
Very fast.

Opening up my presents
Pleased everything is here
Then making out my list
Ready for next year.

Matthew Hicks (13)
Ashfield Boys' High School

Hallowe'en Scares

In the misty night ghouls come out to play.
Snarling, roaring, jumping, looking for you.
Ghosts float round rattling their chains going
Through walls in search of their lost things.
Zombies pop out of nowhere.
Oh no!
They've got me!

Lee Thompson (11)
Ashfield Boys' High School

School Of Scares

A dark, scary morning,
A dog barking far in the distance,
The heavens falling, thunder and lightning,
The dark school gates,
The entrance, dark and black,
The creepy, dark corridor,
It makes you want to turn back.

The teachers don't care,
They just leave you sitting there,
The teachers always yell,
You feel like you're in Hell,
In the dining hall they feed you fish,
It's almost as bad as learning English.

Six hours a day,
They take your life away,
They make your life a living hell,
And then you hear the bell.

You feel you want to pray,
It's finally the end of the day.

Chris Rafferty (13)
Ashfield Boys' High School

School No! A Nursery School

Here I am at my nursery school.
Knowing I would act the fool.
There's the other new kid.
He ran and hid.
He's away to play with the building tool.

When he walked up there.
He was covered up to his hair.
He was filling his cup up to the brim.
He looked a little grim.
I knew it was because he had a tear.

Jonathan McCaughan (13)
Ashfield Boys' High School

The Spooky Party

The spooks are off to a ball,
Which is held in a haunted hall.
They all dance by the moonlight,
Have you ever seen such a spooky sight?

They shake their bones in tune to the band,
And rattle and wave their hands
There's a ghost with his head tucked under his arm
And he can feed it without causing alarm.

The skeletons and goblins dance and laugh,
While the ghosts fly and eat
The morning is now and the party must stop,
Will you see them tonight?
Well you just might.

Andrew Rooney (11)
Ashfield Boys' High School

My Poem

One day a group of us went to the pool,
A big lad was there, acting the fool.
I pretended to be cocky and cool,
When really I wanted to hide in the pool.

After pushing and shoving like a big nancy,
Along came his sister who I could quite fancy.
Out of the pool we all did run,
As it wasn't my idea of having fun.

Out came my mobile to make a quick call,
Just as the big lad ran into the wall.
Ducking and diving we ran to the hall,
Wasn't I lucky I made that quick call.

Craig Holmes (13)
Ashfield Boys' High School

Delicious Fish

Fish from the chip shop
Tasty and delicious
Crunchy in some places
And munchy as well.

Scampi is lovely,
Tiny, tasty,
Slimy, chewy and
Delicious and juicy.

Fish fillets with lots of vegetables,
Cheese and all sorts of sauces
Put in baps, all piled up.
Crunching through and munching too
All fish are always delicious.

Richard Lewis (11)
Ashfield Boys' High School

A Poor Snowman

Boring
Made of snow
A scarf carrot
All of that
Children like it
You say you want to be one
Think again
And in a couple of days
The snowman has melted
I know this because
I was one
I melted and nobody cared
Not a memory
Absolutely nothing.

Ryan Stirling (12)
Ashfield Boys' High School

American Burgers

American burgers are different from what you get here
American burgers aren't like any other burgers
They are so juicy and greasy
The steamy goodness wafting through the kitchen door
The chef flipping the patty
The patty hitting the grill
You can even hear the zzzizzle
Cooked to perfection
Delicious melting cheese on top
Vinegar coated gherkins
Served on a tray
Pots of ketchup and mustard
A drink of Coke
A plate of French fries
Mmmmmmmm
Biting a large mouthful
Teeth sinking through
The cheese
The gherkins
The ketchup and mustard
The patty
The bun
The delectable taste running down my throat
A mouthful of French fries
A gulp of Coke
Deeeelicious
Argh!
'Mum, may I have another?'
'No!'

Michael Carey (11)
Ashfield Boys' High School

Power!

Power here
Power there
Power everywhere
This one wants this job
And the other another.
At the end of it all
They probably won't get the job.
Why?
They never seem to see
What the job has to offer.
All they see is the pound signs
And they're after it.
But why is it pound signs?
Why do they not look
And see what's on offer?

Andrew Steed (15)
Ashfield Boys' High School

Big Mac Meal

Big Mac you are so dreamy
And look so creamy
With all the sauce
You are the boss.
You are so munchy
And all so crunchy
That you are yummy
In my tummy.
All the juice and flavour is so good,
The Big Mac Meal makes good food.
The fries are thin
And drip on my chin.
When I finish
I put the rubbish in the bin.

Mark Irvine (11)
Ashfield Boys' High School

I Love Pizza

When we order it I jump about
Like I've just escaped from the nut house.
I get so excited.
My favourite place is Pizza Hut.
I love just hearing it,
The crunching of the crust,
Its sizzling cheese,
Makes my mouth water.
When it comes I lift it
And take a bite,
Without getting a plate.
When I bite into it
I feel like I've got
To get tucked in.
I mean,
It even smells heavenly.

Bradley Dodds (11)
Ashfield Boys' High School

There Is A Witch

There is a witch
At the top of my street,
She has a funny nose
And really smelly feet.
She has a green face
And a big, hairy mole
And when you look at it,
She casts a spell
And turns you into a girl called Nicole.
She has a black cat
That gives you a fright
And it only comes out in the middle of the night.
It is black from head to toe
And where it is, nobody knows.

David Docherty (11)
Ashfield Boys' High School

Why Terrorism?

Why terrorism? Why Iraq?
Why death? Why war?
Why are soldiers going to fight?
Soldiers that might not make it back before night.

Presidents talking about peace,
When all they want is war.
Why do they talk this talk?
Why war? Why Iraq?

People screaming aloud,
Because their son has died.
People going to fight,
For what? Peace?

Why terrorism? Why death?
Are these people sane?
Who thinks killing is right?
Why terrorism? Why Iraq?

Andrew Ellison (15)
Ashfield Boys' High School

Immature

After a while you start getting old,
At least that's what I've been told.
As you get older you become more mature about this,
I'm really not sure.
Some people will be immature forever,
Laughing at friends and things altogether.
They'll laugh at people whenever they fall,
They'll also laugh at the freakishly tall.
They'll laugh at cartoons and act like 'spoons',
Even get on like a right set of goons.
But some people are just immature you see,
Now, that's enough about me!

Ryan Tate (15)
Ashfield Boys' High School

Delicious Ribs In Honey Sauce

When my mum orders it from the Chinese
I run upstairs in excitement.
When it comes I smell it,
Run downstairs and open the bag in excitement.
I don't wait for a plate,
I open the tub and get tucked in.
Ribs
It feels rough when I lift it,
I bite into it, I slurp,
I lift up my head
And let the smooth piece of meat
Slide down my throat,
Trying not to choke.
All the honey sauce goes over my lips
I lick my lips, take a drink of Coke
And started all over again.

Daryl Finlay (11)
Ashfield Boys' High School

Food

The word food,
Kind of puts me in the mood
For a big ham bap.
As I give the man the money,
He says do not snap,
But just then the wind blew off my cap.
I run and I drop the ham bap,
My money falls into a bunch of old dolls.
Just then I stop and think,
I've lost my ham bap,
My money and my cap.
I'll think twice before I buy a ham bap.

Michael Sewell (13)
Ashfield Boys' High School

The Pastie Supper

It calls my name as I stand in the queue,
I say I want to get something new.
What about a battered sausage or a chicken breast?
It says, 'You'll have a pastie supper so forget all the rest.'

The woman at the counter asks what I want.
I say, 'I'll have a pastie supper covered with salt.'

I run back down the street,
I want to get home so I can eat.
When I open the door I can't wait no more,
I put it on a plate, it's time for the pastie supper
To take its fate.

I get it down me as fast as I can,
Then wash it down with Coke in a can.

So after I've finished I'm really full,
I think about getting another one,
But my mum says you're only allowed one,
That is the rule.

Kyle Young (12)
Ashfield Boys' High School

My Nose

I did not pick this nose,
that gives me my distinct pose.
So when I laugh, people see,
that my nose embarrasses me.
I don't know whether to laugh or cry,
but either way I end up shy.
So when I pout and start to cry
and a tear runs from my eye, I shout . . .
I don't really, this poem's a lie!

Nathan Dickson (15)
Ashfield Boys' High School

Ice Cream

The ice cream I eat
Is a wonderful treat
The mint flavour is so crunchy
And the normal flavour is so munchy
Vanilla flavour looks like snow
And when I eat it, my heart rate grows.

It feels so horribly soft
And the coldness could freeze my tongue
The bubble flavour is as blue as the sky
The chocolate flavour always makes me want to fly.

When I eat it, it tastes so good,
That my tongue does a boogie woogie dance.
The strawberry flavour is so good
That sometimes I nearly die of too much pleasure
Mmm, mmmmm . . .

Gerald Taulo (11)
Ashfield Boys' High School

Food Flying All Around

Food flying all around,
Zooming, zooming to the crowd.
People hurling all types of food,
Potatoes, carrots and Brussels sprouts, oh puke,
Rice, tomatoes, oh look
An orange zooming to a man's back
And hits the man with a giant smack.
He was looking all about
And saw the boy who hit the man
With an orange zooming to the back
And hit the man with a giant smack,
So that's the end of our tale
And the boy began to wail and wail!

Matthew Wightman (11)
Ashfield Boys' High School

The Successful Rap

I hate school, school hates me
I'd rather be home watchin' TV
'Cause maths and English just ain't me
'Cause I'm a rapper can't you see?

I'd rather be home writin' a song
Instead of gettin' questions wrong,
So let me drop out of school
And everything will be cool,
So goodbye A-levels and GCSEs
Because I'm away to watch TV.

No don't do dat, don't be a fool
'Cause droppin' school's not one bit cool.
Don't throw away your life and career
When success is so very near,
So do your A-levels and GCSEs
And one of these days you will thank me!

Matthew Brown (12)
Ashfield Boys' High School

Food Chain

F ood comes here, food comes there, food is from everywhere.
O ther places, other roads, other things that food may show.
O f all the places food may grow, they have been to our countries so.
D o they grow under the ground? Or do they grow on the trees?

C ome and see all the food, from all over the world.
H ave some fruit, have some veg, have some food that's on the tree
   on the ledge.
A nd when you do you'll need the loo so don't eat all the food.
 I n the store at night, all the food is a fright.
N ow the story ends right here, so go and have a bit of glory.

Daniel Mills (13)
Ashfield Boys' High School

A Tuesday School Day

I wake up drowsily at eight,
I think about the food soon on my plate.
I then get a shower,
I wish I could have an hour.
My mum makes me bacon rashers,
After that I clean my nashers.

I then get dressed,
I hope my teachers will be impressed.

When I arrive at school,
I am glad because the DJ on the radio talks a lot of drool.
I go to registration class,
I say to myself, 'I'd love a can of Shandy Bass.'

Then we go to science, where we use Bunsen burners,
But if not used right, it could make your hair go up like Tina Turner's.
We then get ten minutes for our break,
That's how long it will take.

We then go to geography where we learn about maps,
If anyone talks, they get a few slaps.
We then go to maths where my fingers go numb,
From counting them and my thumb.

We then get PE, where we kick a football up and down the hall,
We then get lunch where I hang about with a bunch.

After lunch we go to life and work where we learnt about a justice clerk.
We then go to English where I am sneezing,
Because the window is open and it is freezing.

We then go to French,
Where somebody lets off a stench!

The bell is ringing
And I feel like singing.

I bet you didn't know I was a poet
And now everyone will know it.

Stuart Campton (13)
Ashfield Boys' High School

My Special Dream

When I lay down to sleep
No nightmares come to my head.
I'm so quiet when I sleep,
I have good dreams of places
I have never been before.
Dreams of magic in the air,
Of strange animals and creatures,
Of nice places.
Dreams of peace and calm,
Of beauty and of love
Where people care about each other.
No worries, no bullies and no wars,
No weapons or harm,
No schoolwork or homework,
Then my world falls apart,
I wake up!

Jamie Reid (12)
Ashfield Boys' High School

Shadows Of Death

The roaring of the engine,
The light of the air bombs,
The flash! It hurts my eyes
But then it all goes quiet.

Is it over?
Open the door and see.
I scream, the house is gone,
The Germans took our home.

Bricks lying everywhere,
Can't see anyone,
Not here, nor there,
Just the deafening sound of silence.

Mark Watty (13)
Ashfield Boys' High School

The Hamster

The hamster is the boss in my house
That little ball of fur,
He sits with his eyes glaring
And teeth he likes to bare.

The hamster is the boss in my house,
He only likes me.
When Mum and Dad go near him
He goes mental-ly.

The hamster is the boss in my house,
He hates my sister too,
When she tries to stroke him
He bites because that is all he can do!

The hamster used to be the boss in my house,
I loved him so much,
But hamsters only live for a year or two,
So now I don't know what we will do!

Christopher McDowell (13)
Ashfield Boys' High School

Horror Of War

Men marching on to war,
Not knowing what's in store.
Women watching proudly on
Waving flags high.

Men went on to trenches,
No glory to find,
Only blood, guts and gore,
What a terrible time!

Women hear the sirens,
Knowing what's to come.
The smell, noise and fear,
Oh, what a terrible time.

Steven Browne (13)
Ashfield Boys' High School

The Taste Of Freedom

In the darkness I wait
For the fool who awakens me,
Then I will go through the gate
And finally I'll be free.

And when I escape from this prison
I will take my revenge,
On the fools that locked me here
And my friend will be avenged.

Then I shall fulfil my true potential
And take over the world,
The countries will fall one by one
Like objects in the way of a tornado.

And when it is all over
And I am in control,
I shall start life on other planets
For that is my real goal!

Graeme Stevenson (14)
Ashfield Boys' High School

Tombstone Poetry In 1964

In 1964 Freddy had a war,
He fought all day, he fought all night,
He fought with all his strength and might.
He had a sword,
He killed a man,
All over a slice of ham,
Until one day he was struck by a knife.
Guess who it was? His cunning wife,
So now he's reached a horrid death,
To go and feel the Devil's breath.

Matthew Tipping (13)
Ashfield Boys' High School

Lizard Food

Lizard food is horrible
Because it's living insects!
Eww! Yuk!
I think it would taste like duck!
Because I hate insects and ducks,
Yuk! Yuk! Yuukk!

Lizard food is horrible
Because it's living crickets!
Eww! Yuk!
I think it would feel like losing a wicket
Because I hate crickets and losing wickets.
Yuk! Yuk! Yuukk!

Lizard food is horrible
Because it's living moths.
Eww! Yuk!
I think it would feel like cloths
Because I hate moths and cloths.
Yuk! Yuk! Yuukk!

Joshua Smyth (12)
Ashfield Boys' High School

My Giraffe

My giraffe so big and tall.
Dear giraffe touching the sky,
Giraffe I say how hot is it up there?
With your neck so long and dangly
Can you see our house from there?
Dear giraffe most of your brothers
And sisters are behind bars.
Dear giraffe would you like some hay?
Dear giraffe so big and tall,
Was there ever a bigger animal than you?

David Hodson (11)
Ashfield Boys' High School

Slipped Away

I miss you,
I miss you so bad,
I don't forget you,
Oh it's so sad,
I hope you can hear me,
'Cause I remember it clearly,
That day you slipped away,
Was the day that I found,
It wouldn't be the same,
Each day without you,
Makes me want to cry,
I didn't get around to kiss you,
Goodbye on the hand,
I've had my wake-up,
Won't you wake-up,
I keep asking why,
I can't take it,
It wasn't fake,
It happened, you passed away.

Chris Boyd (14)
Ashfield Boys' High School

Sweetcorn

S weet, sugary taste,
W atery at first,
E mpty onto a plate,
E at all you can,
T he texture is smooth,
C ould be crunchy,
O h I love it,
R eally tasty,
N ot at all bad.

Kristian Bloomer (11)
Ashfield Boys' High School

Universe

The sun, moon, Earth and stars,
Jupiter, Venus, Pluto 'n' Mars,
Why do the stars shine so bright
Especially in the dark of night?

Black holes
Suck up our souls,
What's happening here?
Oh dear! Oh dear!

No gravity at all,
No atmosphere,
Freaking out with panic and fear.

The moon shining so bright
Lighting up the dark, dark night,
Oh what a universe!
Oh what a universe!

Martyn Cummings (14)
Ashfield Boys' High School

Hallowe'en

Hallowe'en is so much fun,
Dressing up and making masks.
Fake sword, fake fangs,
Goblets and lighting pumpkins.

Hallowe'en with fireworks,
Bright and not just one.
Many different colours
Lighting up the noisy sky.

Hallowe'en fancy dress,
After trick or treating
With Frankenstein and the mummy,
Witches, ghosts, goblins and ghouls.

Mark McCann (11)
Ashfield Boys' High School

Soldier

The toys of death are spitting lead
And the red of blood is finally freed
As the sun shines on the faces of grief
The wake of rest is finally quick.

The sound of shackles, chains and cuffs
Rhyme to the tune of horror's truth
And the people are crying, 'Set us free'
As well as the beat of war coming through.

The pulse of fear is pumping seeds
To release the troopers' inevitable good deeds,
Democracy and disgrace is brought upon one's mind
To encourage life and deaths of mankind.

As he jumps out of the mud-filled trench
He kills men for his own blood quench,
The gun drops, as well he kneels
As he stares with sorrow towards his own death shells.

Now he knows what pain he's brought
And with the mind of hope and courage he's fought.

Robert Douglas (14)
Ashfield Boys' High School

Fruit

Fruit comes in all different shapes and sizes,
Different colours too,
Some nice, some not,
It is healthy for me and you.
You can eat fruit anywhere, anywhere at all,
You can grow fruit yourself, if you take care of them
You could end up with delicious fruit at your fingertips.

Ryan Hamilton (11)
Ashfield Boys' High School

My Trip With An Alien

My mum told me a story one night,
That story really gave me a fright.
My eyes popped out of my head,
When she told me an alien was under my bed.

Just before I went to sleep,
I looked under my bed and had a peep.
I saw a green slimy creature with no hair,
That was the scene that gave me a scare.

A voice said, 'Come with me,'
And I was gone in the count of three.
Next I knew I was off to space,
Now I have left the human race.

I found myself in a street,
No houses, no nothing, just aliens in their bare feet.
Me and an alien had a chat
And he told me about his pet rat.

So my mum would not know I was away,
He was going to send me home (hooray!)
He sent me home the longest route,
That stupid, green, slimy brute.

He sent me home through New York,
Rome, Perth, Zurich and Cork.
At least now I am safely home
And no more stories from my mum.

Simon Laverty (11)
Ashfield Boys' High School

Racing Butterflies

The butterflies before a cross-country race
Are the worst I've ever known!
All the thoughts racing through my mind,
All screaming, *'Win! Win! Win!'*
When I see the tough competition my butterflies
Turn to baby hurricanes!
But I've got a simple list to remember
And if I follow it, I'm guaranteed to win!

I must remember to pace myself and to stay with the crowd!
I've got to remember to keep my eyes open
And not to stray off the track!
I must remember to push myself, all through the race
And extra hard on the home straight!
I've got to remember to *never look back*
When I leave the pack behind!

And if all instructions have been followed well
I must remember to raise my arms up and shout,
When I cross the finish line as the champion!

But at the start of every race, with all the butterflies
I always fail to remember that it's finishing that's important
Not always *winning!*

David Stewart (13)
Ashfield Boys' High School

Chicken Breast

A breast of chicken is my favourite food
With red sauce, it tastes so nice.
With chips and beans it is so good
And for a change I'd like chicken and rice.

Chicken fingers and nuggets too
Are nice but not the best.
Some people eat chicken stew
But my favourite is chicken breast.

Phillip Cooke (11)
Ashfield Boys' High School

The Annoyance

He drives me mad, crazy, up the wall,
interrogating every move or sound,
he has become a burden I long to be rid of,
he's my annoyance.

The passion of wanting to hurt becomes stronger each day,
with the madness and strain he puts me through,
after a good day he spoils the night,
he's my annoyance.

I've reached my breaking point,
why can I not get out?
I tremble lifting my head and finding out he's there,
he's my annoyance.

I quit, I'm out of here,
I grab the blade and in one split second,
in a fraction of a moment
he's no longer my annoyance.

Raymond McClure (14)
Ashfield Boys' High School

Micro Pizza

As I come home on a Monday night from football training
My Micro Pizza awaits me.
As I turn on the microwave
I get myself some orange juice.
Next I await the call for the microwave bell,
Ding! I run for the microwave.
I open the door and take out the pizza,
When I pull it apart the melted cheese stretches like elastic.
It ain't going south it's heading for my mouth,
My teeth crunch into the pizza,
My mouth feels so cheesy,
I'm just trying to take it easy.
I'm so sad that the pleasure is over,
But not for long! There's another one.

Stephen McConnell (11)
Ashfield Boys' High School

The War

The man knew it had to end,
He knew it had started too long ago,
He knew the only way to end it,
The man knew it was time.

The man picked up a black box,
He opened it,
He saw the end of the war,
The man saw a red button.

The codes were entered,
The fingerprint scanned,
The man pushed the button down,
The war was over.

Time seemed to freeze,
Silence in an instant,
Everyone sensed danger,
Then they were gone.

Roger Meaklim (14)
Ashfield Boys' High School

Summer Holidays

Summer holidays here at last,
I'm gonna have a blast,
Lots to do, lots to see,
Lots of fun for you and me.

The sun is hot, my ice cream not,
My friends have come to join the fun.
We love to play all night and day,
But it's time to go.
It's getting late you know
But tomorrow is another
Summer holiday!

Kyle McGarvey (11)
Ashfield Boys' High School

My World

My world is a place of happiness,
My world is a place of peace,
No fighting, no arguments, no wars,
That's what's in my world.

My world has blue skies and green trees,
My world has friends everywhere,
Games rooms, arcades, PlayStation 2s,
That's what's in my world.

My world, I play for Manchester United,
My world, we're top of the league,
Arsenal, Chelsea, Liverpool relegated,
That's what's in my world.

My world, I live in a mansion,
My world, I get sponsored by Nike,
Ferraris, convertibles, football boots too,
That's what I've got in *my world.*

David Quinn (13)
Ashfield Boys' High School

Football Crazy

I love football, it keeps me fit,
I love football, I can't get enough of it.
I play sweeper or centre back,
When the ball comes to me I give it a whack.

I love the feeling you get
When the ball hits the back of the net.
I like when I score free kicks,
That is one of my favourite tricks.

Reece Shaw (11)
Ashfield Boys' High School

Hallowe'en Night

Hallowe'en, a scary night,
It gives me such a freaky fright!
All the kids get their masks,
Waiting for sweets in their bags.

Hallowe'en night, someone came to the door,
Scared me like mad, I fell to the floor.
'Trick or treat?' they said to me.
'Wait till I get up and I'll give you some sweets.'

Hallowe'en, it's nearly gone, *phew!*
I went to the door and *boo!*
'Thanks Mum, I'm really scared now.
That's what I was waiting, on you, to say.'
'It's always freaky son.'
'Ohh! that's great, wow!'
I hate being scared always,
No way!

Craig Campbell (13)
Ashfield Boys' High School

The Best Sandwich

S ticky, slimy sandwiches
A re not very nice,
N either are ones with mustard,
D addy makes his with custard.
W itches ones aren't that nice,
 I make good ones,
C hicken is the best filling,
H am is the worst filling,
E very sandwich has bread,
S o my sandwich has pancakes.

Colin Turnbull (12)
Ashfield Boys' High School

Tennis Shots

I call this shot a top spinner,
I think that it's my first winner.
Andy Roddick just served 156mph, ace!
It flew past me with such pace.

I played Lleyton Hewitt,
He pulled off a beautiful lob.
I was running back, but too slowly,
I felt like a slob.

Playing Tim Henman was a very good game,
All the points were just the same.
He kept playing all the drops,
But the final analysis was a flop!

Tommy Haas plays great all around,
People were betting on him pound for pound!

I was playing all day long,
I didn't get a rest,
But in the end, I played my best!

David Atkinson (13)
Ashfield Boys' High School

Ice Cream

I nfinity's worth of ice creams
C oming towards me, could
E at it down me in minutes.

C ream and custard on the top,
R ed ice cream, brown ice cream, could
E at the lot at once,
A fter tea I will have
M mmm . . . chocolate would be nice.

Andrew Mundy (12)
Ashfield Boys' High School

Rugby

Rugby is a sport.
Every time the referee's shouting,
Giving out penalties,
Waiting for the call,
Waiting for the tackle,
Waiting for the catch.

When the whistle blows
The ball is kicked,
Then the catcher is tackled,
The referee calls,
'Scrum down, bind, hold
And *push!'*

Waiting for the whistle,
Waiting for the tackle,
Waiting for the catch,
Here we go again!

James Malcolm (13)
Ashfield Boys' High School

Autumn

I love to walk among the trees
And watch the falling autumn leaves.
They make a carpet at my feet,
I take my rest and make a seat.

The fruits of the forest fall to the floor,
I watch the birds and squirrels gather their winter store.
The trees show their clawed branches to the sky,
I take my leave and say goodbye.

James Wright (12)
Ashfield Boys' High School

The Day I Sprouted Wings

I'm floating on a cloud,
I'm flying through the air,
I've left behind my worries,
I've forgotten every care.

I'm flying over forests,
I can touch the mountain tops.
As the fields come into view
I can smell the farmer's crops.

I never want to stop,
But the night is close at hand.
It's time for me to lose my wings,
It's time for me to land.

Ben Houston (12)
Ashfield Boys' High School

Food For Thought

Food is good,
Food is fun,
It will give you a big fat bum.

It should taste good,
It should taste great,
You spent all your pocket money on it mate.

You should eat a piece of fruit a day
To keep those calories away.

You will feel better,
You will feel good,
You'll feel the way a real person should.

Adam Letson (13)
Ashfield Boys' High School

The Four Seasons

S un shining weakly
P etals start appearing
R eproduction all around
I ce is disappearing
N ow the weather's getting warmer
G ames are played outside again.

S ummer holidays abroad
U mbrellas are all gone
M any days of endless fun
M oon does not appear 'til late
E veryone is happy now
R ainy days are far away.

A ll the leaves falling
U pon the paths and roads
T rees are bare
U nder grey skies
M onth by month getting colder
N early wintertime.

W indows freezing
I ce on roads
N o more nice days
T o do what I want
E arly nightfall
R aining all day.

Jonathon Bowden (12)
Ashfield Boys' High School

Cars

C ars are cool and go zoom, zoom, zoom
    and most have a lot of room.
A utomatic cars and some are manual,
R ed cars, blue cars, all colour cars,
S peedy cars, slow cars, all the same to me cars.

Andrew Gilmour (12)
Ashfield Boys' High School

Life

Life is fun
and life is sad
My friends and family
are sometimes mad.

Tears are shed
and love is born
There is no time
To sit and scorn.

Growing up
can be hard to do
But growing up
we all must do.

Night has fallen
but the sun will rise
For it's life
it is a big surprise.

Darren Bingham (15)
Ashfield Boys' High School

Hamster's Life

Little hamsters they are so small,
They always look as if they crawl.
When they make their bed of wool,
Sometimes I think they look a fool.
They always forget to fill some gaps,
The sun shines in, I could give them sun caps.
They look at the big figure giving them food,
I am sure they think it is good.
Their legs running on the living room floor,
Chewing on the owner's apple core.
Their eyes and tail make them look like a rat,
I'm sure they would be a good meal for a cat.
But as we still care,
I think a hamster's life is not fair.

Michael Bush (13)
Ashfield Boys' High School

The Wolf's Life

The wolf is born, his life he yearns,
His mother says, 'You have a thing or two to learn.'
She takes him in the snow,
She knows he's very slow.

Three years have slowly passed,
Now he's very fast.
His fur is grey,
In his mouth he has his prey.

Six years have passed,
He's not very fast.
He's now very old,
He looks very cold.

As he dies,
He thinks about those pestering flies.
The natives will know him,
As wolf leader Kwim.

Dean Kerrigan (13)
Ashfield Boys' High School

The Kyber Restaurant

I went to the Kyber Restaurant,
A guy came up
And said, 'What do you want?'
So I looked at the menu
But I couldn't see
Something I fancied for my tea.
The guy recommended masala and peas
But I didn't fancy any of these,
So I ended up with vindaloo
And then I needed to use the loo.
Then the guy said, 'Pay the bill.'
But I said, 'No I feel extremely ill.'

Karl Hutton (12)
Ashfield Boys' High School

Stomach Aches

His pain is unbearable,
His malice is the master,
His thrusting, burning, pulverising destruction
Is all he leaves in his wake.

His churning, crunching spasms of pain,
Make him happy at this game.
He likes to see you wretch and stretch while wriggling on your bed.

His constant torture of the stomach
And his devilish conjuring of pain,
Make him all the better at this terrible game.

His obsolete will of annihilation,
His one purpose in life,
Is to make you feel like you're boking up your intestines.

When the ache is over
And he has left,
Finally you are free of the devil that resided in your chest.

Wayne Clarke (13)
Ashfield Boys' High School

Tornado

The tornado it crashes, bashes and smashes,
It eats cars and swallows people.
It whirls and twirls, as my eyes swirl.

It goes by like a pride of lions,
It would almost make rhythmic sounds.
I cry as my friends go by,
All I want to say is bye bye.

Luke McCall (14)
Ashfield Boys' High School

Soldiers

They don't know what's ahead of them!
They sign up feeling brave
But they're too young to understand
For they're still only young men,
They'll end up in a grave.

Months of training they must endure
To prepare themselves for what's ahead,
Up and down they march and charge,
Obey commands to earn their daily bread.

For war is always round the corner
And soon they will be gone
To fight for their country,
Only God knows, if they will return.

Jonathan Sergeant (14)
Ashfield Boys' High School

Hope

Go west young man! Go west!
The writing's on the wall,
It's for a better future,
I hear the distant call.

But yet I look with hope,
There's so much I can do
To forge this beautiful island.
I'm up for it, are you?

Let's get our act together,
Our future's in our hands.
The youth, they say shall lead us
To find our promised lands.

Tristan Dickey (14)
Ashfield Boys' High School

War

Dying soldiers on the battlefields,
Tanks firing shells at buildings.
Bombshells lying on the ground,
What started such a thing?

Weeping widows left with families,
Helicopters being shot down.
Terrorists rejoicing to live another day,
What started such a thing?

Politicians arguing about what to do,
When they don't do a thing.
It's down to soldiers to win this war,

Man started such a thing!

Mitchell Robb (14)
Ashfield Boys' High School

The Rush

I'm running to school,
I feel such a fool.
I missed the bus
So I have to rush
So I don't get detention,
To write out lines
A thousand times,
To make my hand sore
But they haven't got me this time
Because I am through the door.
I am sure I am on time,
That's brilliant
Just like this rhyme.

Jason Ali (14)
Ashfield Boys' High School

War

Guns rattling, people battling,
The cries of a young man fills the air,
Smoke darkens the sky and blocks the sun,
Clips emptied in an instance,
The same with lives,
These people know *it's war!*

Craters created, bodies unburied,
The steaming lead in someone's leg,
The missing leg of an unlucky fool,
Ten thousand men go in,
Only ten come out,
These people dead in fours.

Barrels blazing, people plastered,
Tanks ordered in, tanks taken out.
Reinforcements have arrived, reinforcements have all died.
No retreat, no surrender, no chance in hell,
The sergeant shouts charge, the sergeant gets killed,
Life is cheap in war.

Michael Boyd (14)
Ashfield Boys' High School

Tollymore Forest Park

As I walked along amongst the trees,
Taking in the fresh breeze,
Peace and tranquillity,
Abating the hectic city life.

Within this place,
All my worries are forgotten,
Dispersed, dispelled into the air,
This is my carefree world.

Jonathan Bevan (14)
Ashfield Boys' High School

Thank You

I need help
But I want fun,
You'll be there
When all's said and done.

You'll stay by me through thick and thin
But I can't tell you what lies within.
You're never to be discarded,
This won't be for the weak-hearted.

There's a lot of things that I could say
But they stay inside me day by day.
I need to let my anger out,
Before I lose it, scream and shout.

I can't describe what happens inside,
But I know for sure that it can't hide.

I want to thank you for helping me through,
I'd be dead if it weren't for you,
I'd be dead if it weren't for you.

Gary Rice (14)
Ashfield Boys' High School

Emotions

What is anger?
Is it a thought?
Is it an action?
Is it a feeling?
If you make it an action,
If you act in anger
Then you must always play.

What is a thought?
Is it a feeling?
Is it an action
Or does it just help you through the day?

Christopher Higgins (14)
Ashfield Boys' High School

Universe

The sun, moon, Earth and stars,
Jupiter, Venus, Pluto and Mars.

The light of the moon on a dark night,
Shining, shining very bright.
It lights up the streets, the valley too,
The light shining on me and you.

The stars shining bright making pictures in the night
And when you die and go up high,
You may have a picture in the sky.

The sun's the brightest of them all,
It makes you hot and very warm,
The animals scream and shout once they see the sun is out.
It makes you get out of bed
And go to work until the end.

Jupiter, Venus, Pluto and Mars
Are all up high beyond the stars.

No gravity at all,
No atmosphere,
Scared and alone, full of fear.

It's time for me to say goodbye
And come down from way up high.

Kyle Young (14)
Ashfield Boys' High School

Fireworks

It is Hallowe'en night
And the moon is shining bright,
New colourful fireworks going up into the sky,
The louder they sound, the higher they fly.
Some people walking past, who don't have a clue,
Look into the sky with an ah, ah, ooh.
There are kids enjoying themselves going trick or treating,
If you call down Abigail Road you might get a beating.

Mark Roulston (14)
Ashfield Boys' High School

Hallowe'en On The 12th Of July

Orange and yellow flames flying high,
Is it Hallowe'en or the 12th of July?

Lots of kids trick or treating,
Or the bands playing and the crowds singing.

The crowds whistling to the band's tune,
Or the kids screaming to the big frightening gloom.

Flags flying high red, white and blue,
Or kids screaming blue murder too.

There you see the marchers walk past,
Or see the kids with the scary masks.

Drums banging, band sticks in the air,
Or kids wearing masks with creepy hair.

Orange and yellow flames flying high,
Is it Hallowe'en or the 12th of July?

Scott Mercer (13)
Ashfield Boys' High School

Drugs

I'm the killer,
The main thriller,
Not a week goes by,
Without a cry,
Lying and stealing,
Just to get that feeling,
I will make you become abusive,
To everyone that matters,
I'm an addiction you'll
Find hard to beat,
Don't start something you can't control,
Walk away with your body, mind and soul.

Chris Morton (14)
Ashfield Boys' High School

Rugby

Rugby is a tough sport,
Rugby is a physical sport,
In rugby I play forward,
Sometimes I get injured,
I score tries and tackle people.
My team is always winning and I can't stop grinning.
My favourite player is Brian O'Driscol, who plays for Ireland.
In rugby I get dirty from head to toe,
I sometimes lose my temper,
But rugby is my favourite sport.
Rugby is my favourite sport because I like the way
It separates the men from the boys.
I like the way it is tough and shows your fitness.
It's good the way you can score tries by doing special skills
Like side stepping and reverse passes.
That's why I like rugby.

Conor McCrory (14)
Ashfield Boys' High School

Abuse

Happy on the outside, though weeping on the inside,
Working hard at school though belted at home.
Hiding in the corner waiting, waiting . . .
Door opening loudly, he chants,
Nothing to do but wait, wait,
Banging up the stairs getting louder and louder
The more the sweat drips off her head,
A big loud crash as he falls to the ground,
A sound of glass smashing,
Enter the room blaming it on her, hits her, kicks her
Laughing, laughing.

Stephen Turkington (14)
Ashfield Boys' High School

My Dad's Snoring

I wake up,
It's the middle of the night.
Oh no, I need to go to the toilet!
It's miles downstairs,
What's that?
A pig snorting?
No, my dad's snoring!
The floorboard creaks,
A loud ghostly groan comes from my brother's room . . .
I have to stop and listen,
There is silence. I take a step . . . step . . . step . . .
Argh! I bang my knee on a table.
I hear footsteps,
They're coming from my mum and dad's room.
I hide in the towel cupboard.
I'm very near the toilet now, only a few steps to go.
It's my dad, he goes into the bathroom.
The toilet seat goes down.
What's that? Oh no, my dad's snoring!
It's not fair,
It's the middle of the night
And I really need to go!

Michael McGibney (13)
Ashfield Boys' High School

Autumn Breeze

Autumn leaves fall off the trees,
Twisting, turning in the breeze,
As they fall to the ground,
They form a carpet all around,
As I walk through these leaves,
I can feel the autumn breeze.

Mark Wallace (13)
Ashfield Boys' High School

Fall Of The Sniper

It's 9.15 in the morning
And people are going to die.
It's time they all learnt a lesson,
Those punks are going to fly.

I pick them off one by one,
I used my sniper rifle gun.
Its muzzle was silenced,
They don't know where it came from.

Someone's seen me, I better run,
I leave the gun and run.
I try to make for the door
And trip over my shoelace.

I get out the door and hear sirens,
The police are closing in.
I run for the fire escape
Only to find it's been locked.

I run downstairs,
It's hell down there
And then I get shot in the back,
I fall face first in a pool of cold blood.

I roll over only to have a torch shone in my face,
I notice the face to be a mate of mine.
He shot me in the back
And now I'm going to die.

Michael McIlhatton (14)
Ashfield Boys' High School

United Kingdom Limericks

There was a guy from Liverpool
who thought he was really cool.
He then saw a girl,
he asked her to twirl
and now he has started to drool.

There was a woman from London
she knew there was work to be done.
She saw a grass snake,
then hit it with a rake
and now she thinks she is fun.

There was a guy from Blackpool
who acted like a fool.
He went to Spain,
it started to rain,
and he nearly got killed by a bull!

There was a girl from Glasgow
who thought she would never grow.
She went to France,
she was ordered to dance
and now she's bigger than Tore Andre Flo.

There was a couple from Belfast
who thought they were really fast.
They went on a boat,
it didn't float
and now they've broken the mast.

Ian Boal (13)
Ashfield Boys' High School

Fruit

Fruit is all around us,
It's everywhere we look,
It's hidden in our cupboards
Or stuffed behind a book.

There's all kinds of different fruit,
A pear, a peach, a plum.
Do not eat loads of pizzas
They go straight to your bum.

So many fruits to pick from,
So much fruit to crunch,
At least we know, in this big world
There's plenty of fruit to munch.

Fruit is very good for you
As I hope you know.
Fruit will fill us full of strength
And help our bones to grow.

Craig Reynolds (13)
Ashfield Boys' High School

Feet

Feet are so repulsive,
Cleaning them should be compulsive.
They smell like cheese,
So take them from my nose please.
Some big, that means big shoes,
Some small, that means small shoes.
I'll tell you what else smells, socks,
Although I'll leave that for another time,
And leave it to another rhyme.

Aaron Moffatt (16)
Ashfield Boys' High School

Spellings For A Dyslexic

Spellings
Are such horrid things,
You learn them long,
You learn them hard,
Syllable, by syllable, by syllable.

Each week new ones come,
Each week ten come,
Four days a week to learn,
Three, by four, by three,
Then all.

Once you've learnt them
There's the test
Nerves racking all the time,
She calls them out,
One, by one, by one.

It's over!
It's done!
And then it starts
All over again . . .

William Ashenhurst (13)
Ashfield Boys' High School

The Horrors Of War

Soldiers battle, families in shock,
Soldiers on beaches, families eating rations,
Soldiers in the air, families being bombed,
Soldiers on the sea,
The horrors of war.

Soldiers dying, people dying,
Trench dug, bombers down,
Bullets flying all around,
The horror of war.

Kyle Stewart (13)
Ashfield Boys' High School

Hallowe'en

Moonlight, starlight, the bogeyman's coming out tonight,
Give us a candle, give us a light,
If you don't you'll get a fright,
It's Hallowe'en night,
Trick or treat,
Smell your feet,
It's Hallowe'en night!

Witches, wizards, goblins and ghouls,
The kids are out so give a shout,
It's Hallowe'en night!
The witches' spells smell like fungus from your toe,
Because of your grandpa Joe.
It's Hallowe'en, Hallowe'en,
It's Hallowe'en night!

Ian Jones (13)
Ashfield Boys' High School

My Pet

I have a pet dog called Bob,
He is a bit of a slob.
He lies on the chair,
And his hair goes everywhere.

He barks all day and barks all night,
He gives my sister a bit of a fright.
I let him out the back,
He gives my neighbour a heart attack.

I go out in the morning,
The dog is gone,
And the gate is open, where could he be?
I'm just hoping he will come back to me.

Curtis Livingstone (13)
Ashfield Boys' High School

Field Of Dreams

Every city has its heroes
Every city has its zeroes
I'm going to be a someone
Not a no one.

Football crazy, immensely insane
Guess you can say I'm pretty vain
City boy with a huge big ego
Maybe one day I'll play like 'Figo'.

Hard work, talent and dedication
Some day I'll be the talk of the nation
Pele, Bestie, they had style . . .
I think I'd outplay them by a mile.

The green-field of dreams is my goal
Not just to be on the dole
From the stands the crowd will sing and chant
That's when I'll know I've got what I want!

Tony Mills (13)
Ashfield Boys' High School

Chips

Chips are my favourite food,
I think they taste so very good.
If you put them on a plate,
I'll be sure they'll all be ate.
At lunch time if there's a choice,
It's chips for me and more, rejoice!
But when I am eating them at home,
I make sure that I'm alone.
As I said before,
These chips are good,
'Specially the way Dad makes them,
That is why they are my favourite food.

Michael Baxter (13)
Ashfield Boys' High School

Christmas

Boys,
Girls,
Mums,
And dads,
They all love Christmas.

Boys get cars,
Girls get dolls,
Mums and dads get presents.

Girls and boys go out to play,
Whilst mums and dads make dinner.

Christmas dinner is on the table,
Turkey,
Pudding,
Stuffing,
And sprouts.

They grab their cracker and pull,
Bang!
More toys fall out,
A small keyring,
A small frame,
Jokes to tell and hats to wear.

I wish it was Christmas Day,
So I could mess around and play.

Christmas is the special time of the year!

Glen Matthews (13)
Ashfield Boys' High School

Soldier

Gold in colour
But these are not treasure
Murderous bullets from me, a fearful soldier
Crouched in mud
Ankle-deep
Like a prisoner I'm held
No movement, no choice
Keep fighting, scattering more fool's gold.

A fog of dust from collapsed buildings
Firing into the midst is the only attack
Like shooting fish in a barrel
Pointless
The scattered bodies' rotting, rancid stench
Is this what we're fighting for? Death?
Losing faith, we're fighting a losing battle
Hatred to the enemies.

I smell fear over the rotting corpses
All my senses are blocked
Overloaded by everything
I break down in a mess
I'm now dumb
Hollow
Exposed to what I really am
Afraid, alone.

Graham Moorhead (15)
Ashfield Boys' High School

My Poem About Carla

I went to the Icebowl
On Saturday night,
When I got to the door
I saw my girlfriend Carla.
In the Icebowl that night
Was a massive big fight,
It was even on the news,
But I didn't mind
Because I had Carla
Standing beside me.
I am so lucky to be
Going out with her,
Because she is so nice and kind.
It's her birthday on Monday,
I'm going to buy her a ring.
Everything's all right
When Carla's in sight.

Andrew Gray (13)
Ashfield Boys' High School

My Dog Buster

When I come home from school
I am met at the door
By this tiny, little brown thing
Which I really do adore.
He runs round and round,
This tiny little pup,
He won't settle down
Until I lift him up.
I would really miss him
If he wasn't there,
But I will always look after him
Because I really care.

Karl Spence (13)
Ashfield Boys' High School

Curry Chip Poem

Curry and chips
Oh what a trip
Cannot complain
No more pain.

My mouth's dry
I am about to cry
I like them hot
With lots of salt.

Now in my mouth
It is going down south
What a great taste
None gone to waste.

Not being rude
But this curry food
Was definitely too good.

Scott McVitty (13)
Ashfield Boys' High School

Hippo

Hungry, hungry hippo,
Where do I go?
No river to swim slow
I'm a hungry hippo
Only got this trough
To keep my skin damp
Oh I wish I could go home.

Hungry, hungry hippo
I hate the snow
Shouldn't be on this island
Because I am too cold
Hungry, hungry hippo
I hate the snow.

Jamie Reid (16)
Ashfield Boys' High School

Hospitals

Hospitals seem to be really big,
But when you get inside one,
It always seems to be bombarded.

Hospitals seem to be full of misery,
But the nurses always seem
To try and lighten things up.

The Ulster Hospital is warm,
The City Hospital is cold,
I wish there was one
That was just right.

Hospital food is really, really bad,
You just wish you could have a takeaway.

The only thing good about hospitals
Is that most of the time
You come out better than you went in.

But in my case,
I went in with a broken leg,
And out I came with an infected leg.

Neil Carter (16)
Ashfield Boys' High School

Horror Of War

B ombs flying overhead
L ots of shelters
A lot of deaths
C ollection of debris
K nowing your friend's house has been hit.
O ut of the sky the bombs fall
U nusual noises and screams
T he sound of sirens.

Ben McKay (13)
Ashfield Boys' High School

The Story Of Skins And Prime

There was an old man called Skins,
Who loved to look in bins,
He often found tins and old fish fins,
But that didn't stop him looking in bins.

Skins had a mate called Prime,
Who never got to work on time,
So he didn't earn a dime.
So he decided to commit a crime,
He planned it out fine,
He even painted his face pine.

But the men still said the money was mine,
So Prime said fine and to this day he still doesn't earn a dime.
So that's what will happen to you
If you don't get to work on time.

Richard Kerry (15)
Ashfield Boys' High School

My Sports

The football is passed to me at last,
I'm running down the wing so fast.
I blast the ball, I hope I score,
It goes in, the crowd all roar.

Hockey is a very fast game,
Getting the ball in the net is the aim.
Round the players the movement is slick,
The ball holding tight to the back of the stick.

Seven foot high is the basketball net,
The ball is in the hands of an expert I bet.
He shoots, he aims right at the hoop,
Oh what a throw - it's an Ally-oop.

Alan Alexander (13)
Ashfield Boys' High School

My Naughty Little Cousin

My naughty little cousin
Was five the other day
She went to Indiana Land
With all her friends to play.

They all climbed up the slides
And pushed each other in
Among the coloured balls
My little cousin's head did spin.

They swung on the ropes like apes
And soon they all fell down
They got up and ran away
Laughing like circus clowns.

Then my naughty little cousin
Fell and bumped her head
Cried like a baby
And showed me where it bled.

She said she thought she'd broken it
Which we didn't think was true
But then all the wailing stopped
When Mum said, 'Here, have a chew.'

Peter Law (12)
Ashfield Boys' High School

Have You Ever Seen A Dragon?

Have you ever seen a dragon?
I have
Round the corner at the old bridge
Anyone who goes round there at night
Would get eaten up.

They have lived there for years
And kids have been left in tears
When their parents don't come back
From doing their shopping.

Ryan Allman (13)
Ashfield Boys' High School

Despair

I am on my own again
Darkness arrives
Street lights appear
Streets all deserted
No one about
Just me and that grubby old doorway
Nothing to do but sit here and think
I fall asleep
Cold and damp
Just some newspapers to lie on
And an old torn sleeping bag
Next morning as usual
Trying to beg for money
To get something to eat
To keep me going for a while
Why do I bother?

Graham Darragh (16)
Ashfield Boys' High School

Our Wee Country

Our wee country does us proud,
When the supporters roar so loud,
From Taylor to Smith they're all brave souls,
We just hope Healy will score us some goals.

That night in Cardiff the Ulstermen roared,
No one believed when Healy had scored,
When that goal went in we were two-nil up,
Now we're on our way to the World Cup!

Last night was great,
We didn't get beaten,
It finished 3-3,
Now we're full of glee.

Brett McMaster (16)
Ashfield Boys' High School

Portugal, Euro 2004

For almost a year
We scrimped and saved
Then the big day came
And to all we waved . . . goodbye.

We journeyed by coach
Then flew over the sea
At last we arrived
Where we wanted to be . . . actually.

A few days to relax
Then at last the coach came
Overcome with excitement, we travelled
To see our first big game . . . couldn't believe it.

Germany vs Holland, Croatia vs Switzerland
Italy played twice and Sweden we saw
But although the games were exciting
They all ended in a draw . . . imagine!

Too soon the holiday ended
As we stepped onto the plane
But I don't think I'll ever see
Anything like Euro 2004 again . . . maybe the World Cup!

Michael Reynolds (12)
Ashfield Boys' High School

Manchester United

Manchester United are the best team,
Winning seems to be their dream.
They love to win and hate to lose,
United are the best team.

Manchester United are the best team,
They always seem to score.
And when they do the crowds just roar
And roar!

Michael Stewart (15)
Ashfield Boys' High School

The Sad Circus

Back and forth that's all I do,
I'd rather be in the zoo.
People shriek and stare at me,
Usually they are scared of me.

There is a nasty man I just can't stand,
He beats me with sticks and bars.
Other animals pray
And I just say,
'Put me back in the wild
So I can hear the rivers flow
Back then I had somewhere to go.'

If that ever happened,
You could never imagine,
How happy I would be.

Jason McCann (15)
Ashfield Boys' High School

The Wild Tiger

I was once a wild animal and an athletic animal,
I used to roam the land,
Now I roam nothing
I came from the jungle to the cage
Now I'm in a rage!

I got caught roaming the land,
I got caught by catchers,
Now all I see are watchers.
People come and see me
But they don't know that I have been here for years.
Now all I do is sit in this cage
Watching the days go by, rage by rage!

Michael McClean (15)
Ashfield Boys' High School

The Shore

The shingle beach,
the tide rolls in,
it wets shells and sand alike,
it travels all the way up to the shore.

The twigs blow on the soft white sand,
the seaweed looking lost and dead,
the beach is empty
except for a dog running
along the shoreline.

Oh to be summer when the beach is full,
the water ever so tempting,
but when winter falls, it brings a curse
and everything is deserted.

No kids with balls,
no ice cream vans,
everywhere is silent,
except for the rushing,
gushing wind.

The night closes in,
the moon shines down
upon the raging sea.
When morning breaks
the raging storm
will have hopefully
passed over.

Andrew Hunter (15)
Ashfield Boys' High School

My Old Cat

My old cat is called Henry,
he is the best cat you could ever have,
He sits on my lap
And has a nice nap
And doesn't wake up till the morning.

I come downstairs,
And stroke his hairs
And brush him and put him outside.
When he comes in
I give him some food
And he'll eat and eat
As much as he can.

He comes on holidays to Ireland
But not on holidays to Spain
For if he went far
It would cause him some pain.

My old cat is getting tired
I think he should go to bed
Now he should think of tomorrow
And I'll give him tuna instead.
But when I come downstairs
To stroke his lovely hairs
I see he's gone to Heaven
And made happiness there.

Jack Stewart (12)
Ashfield Boys' High School

Teachers

Teachers in my school,
Aren't always cool,
Some can be kind,
Some can be cruel!

Many are smart,
But some can be slow,
How many times
Does Mr Leathem have to shout?
Go! Go! Go!

Gowdy was funny,
Mathers was mad -
Mrs Duffield gives us chocolate,
Aren't we glad.

Some teachers are old,
Some teachers are young,
Cross paths with Mr McMorran,
And you will be hung!

Lewis Cameron (15)
Ashfield Boys' High School

The Rumbling Tum

I see the steam rising from my plate
I want to dig in, just can't wait.
My stomach is hungry for this tasty food
It looks so gorgeous, it smells so good.

I really, really want to eat
It is making my heart beat.
'When will it be ready?' I said
I really, really need to be fed.

My tummy was round, just like Santa
And then I had a gulp of Fanta.
I am full up from all this dinner
My mum, the chef, she's a winner.

Matthew Perry (12)
Ashfield Boys' High School

War

The bombs and grenades are flying
And thousands of people are dying.
Our soldiers are out there trying
To stop their best friends dying.

The boats are coming in
With soldiers ready to run.
As they get off the boats
They hear the enemy's gun.

The planes are flying high
As they drop bombs from the sky.
All the tanks are driving by
This is scary and not a lie.

I have to go and get my lunch
As I have to go out soon.
I hope this war will have ended
Before it robs us of another platoon.

Gareth Brown (12)
Ashfield Boys' High School

Death

Death is all around us
Death is oh so near.

Death stays close to us
It causes chaos and fear.

It makes us kill each other
And call each other names.

But death is with us constantly
We can't control it however hard we try.

So all we can do is live with the thought
Until it knocks at our door.

And we will go to our resting place
Where we will stay for evermore.

Jonathon McIlfatrick (12)
Ashfield Boys' High School

The Football Match!

The match had just begun,
James passed the ball,
He passed the ball to Paul,
Our manager said just to have fun.

Half-time was near,
The other team was full of fear,
The ball was in their net,
They hadn't realised yet.

Five minutes left in the second half,
And all our team began to laugh
We were all sure that we were going to win
And if we didn't our manager was packing it in.

The end of the match had come,
It was time to have lots of fun,
The other team were sad,
But we were glad.

Ben Watton (12)
Ashfield Boys' High School

Pollution

P ollution causes grief all around the world.
O ver the years we have made it worse by releasing smoke
  into the atmosphere
L orries' exhaust fumes rising up into the clean air, black as night.
L ots of fish suffer from careless farmers polluting streams
  with their chemicals.
U p in the sky there is a hole in the ozone layer, which we make
   bigger day by day.
T rees sometimes die covered in acid rain that we have caused.
I n some parts of the world thick clouds of smog cover entire cities.
O il refineries and oil rigs burn fuels that pollute the air we breathe.
N ow everyone realises from the floods and storms that we are
  damaging the world we live in.

What's to be done about pollution?

Gareth Murray (15)
Ashfield Boys' High School

The Haunted House

My heartbeat's fast
Even worse than in the past
Even before I enter
The house of horrors
But when I do
It's worse
The sweat breaks on me
Running down my face like a waterfall down a rock face
I hear the spooky screams
My nerve breaks and I'm off, I start running
Nowhere in particular, just to get away from here
The haunted house was wild
I even had to hold onto my mum's hand
Of course I was a child
Everywhere I look I see things
That frighten me
And make me want to yell
It scares me to hell
It starts to get worse every minute I am there
When I saw the light at the end
I ran and jumped and started rolling towards
The door of light
When I got out I was so pleased
But also embarrassed cause people
Were looking and laughing at me
I didn't really mind
At least I escaped the terror.

Robert McCaughan (15)
Ashfield Boys' High School

My Wonderful Trip

One hot summer day,
Me and my friends went out to play,
When his mum and dad came out to speak to us,
They said, 'Would you like to go camping?
You'll be travelling on a bus.'

When I ran home,
My mum let out a little moan.
I asked, 'Could I go on a trip?'
Then she gave me a little nip.

When we got on the bus,
We were at the back, when someone came and sat beside us,
When the bus stopped, we went for a bite to eat,
When we finished we had to walk and walk, we were beat.

On the second day we hired a boat,
But it barely kept afloat,
Then it started to rain,
It rained so heavily, you could start to feel some pain.

Corey Watson (12)
Ashfield Boys' High School

Me And My Food

Having food whenever I like
Eating crisps with my friend Mike
What can I say food is nice
Especially with chicken fried rice.

Climbing up a really big tree
Then Mum calls, 'Come down for tea.'
A moment of joy rushes to my heart
Because maybe after I could eat a jam tart.

Sausages, pizza, beans and chips
Drinks so big, but taking sips.
All I can think about when I'm hungry, *food!*
Even when I'm in a bad mood.

Adam Turnbull (12)
Ashfield Boys' High School

Poetry Competition

It was a day like all others
I was doing the same old usual thing
But then I was told my uncle had died
I couldn't believe it at first
Astonished, I was devastated
Knowing I would never see him again
I didn't know that last time I saw him would be the last
I felt sorry for my aunt
Wondering how the others are taking it
Driving to the church
Going into the room with the coffin
Hearing everyone cry
Taking a seat in the hall
Listening to the minister
Going outside for the coffin to be buried
Listening to the minister before the coffin gets buried
Then watching the men bury it
Going to my aunt's house
Then taking a moment's silence.

Jamie Laurie (12)
Ashfield Boys' High School

Shivers!

Years ago I saw a witch,
I let out a scream,
She looked so, so mean,
Then I fell into a ditch.

Later on I told my dad,
But he said I was mad,
It's just not fair,
He just doesn't care.

After that, she was in my dreams,
Running about in a pile of beans,
My parents just don't see,
That she is haunting me.

Wayne Carson (12)
Ashfield Boys' High School

Lonely Bill

There was an old woman who was kind,
She had a cat that was blind.
The cat was called Toots,
We thought it was a hoot!

Her house was on a hill,
Her husband's name was Bill.
They sat every day on the window sill,
Until they both got a chill.

The old woman took ill
And so did Bill.
The old woman died,
Bewildered, Bill cried.

Bill was so sad,
People thought he was going mad.
He could not sleep,
All he did was weep.

The day of the funeral it rained,
Everyone's heart filled with pain.
Bill whispered goodbye
And wished he could die.

Michael Adams (12)
Ashfield Boys' High School

Creepy Man

Something that goes
Bump in the night.
A creepy man ran about,
He likes to give people a fright.
He creeps up behind you
And shouts, 'Boo.'
Running down the street in delight
He falls on a step,
Oh no! He's broken his pipe.

Kenneth Comfort (14)
Ashfield Boys' High School

Double, Double, Toil And Trouble

(In the style of Macbeth)

Double, double, toil and trouble,
Fire burns and cauldrons bubble.
An eye of a newt and one smelly foot
Along with her old filthy boots.
The point of whose tail is in Hell?
Name we don't mention, just as well
'And now tonight, we'll have our way,
Once we've finished our evil spell.'
'Ingredients, ingredients,' the witches say.
'And now tonight we'll have our way, oh yay!'

Double, double, toil and trouble
Fire burns and cauldrons bubble.
A toe and a nose that belongs to a bear,
Along with some witch's very long hair.
A witch's broom and then a lizard
(It came from a wand which belongs to a wizard).
Some human insides which they thought was wise
A shell of a snail which is small in size.
One pupil (not a school pupil) from an eye
But now we witches say, 'Goodbye!'

Naomi Gray (11)
Belfast Model School For Girls

Autumn

Leaves so gold, just like a crown,
One by one, they're falling down.
Conkers dropping from the clear blue sky,
I watch the foxes as they pass me by.
The leaves crumble like paper burning in a fire,
Autumn's gifts I do desire.
Shorter days, longer nights,
Autumn scenes, beautiful sights!

Charlotte Howard (11)
Bloomfield Collegiate

Autumn Poem

As I walk up to the bay
I know it's not the month of May.
It's the time of year when the leaves turn red
And the squirrels and badgers go to bed.
The sky above is baby blue,
The leaves are crisp under my shoe.
I hear the scurrying of little feet,
The chilled wind comes by in forceful sheets.

My mouth waters at the smell of apple pie,
Children running happily by.
As my boat bumps upon the shore,
My eyes take in even more.
The rower greets me with a cherry smile and pink cheeks
'All aboard!' I hear him speak.
The boat gracefully glides across the lake
Here and there, a gentle shake.

On the misty bank the tree twigs curl
I step into a different world.
The jagged face of the pumpkin's flicker,
The apples overflow the basket's wicker.
I look up to a scratched door,
Look in to see the noise's core.
I see a table full of sweets
I think to myself, *what a wonderful treat.*

My hand touches a rusty lock
I take one look back at the dock.
I push forward the forbidding door,
People dancing, all twenty-four.

All that night we had fun and danced,
Time was waiting, ready to prance.
Before I knew it, the night was over,
The candles were starting to burn lower.

Sarah Davey (12)
Bloomfield Collegiate

Autumn

A dry autumn morning,
Leaves shining red, gold and brown,
As they fall softly to the ground.
People walking to the sound of
Crunch, crunch, crunch!

I hear squeaking in amongst the leaves,
My dog starts barking as if to say, 'Please!'
Rolling about, searching in the leaves.

I rustle and bustle amongst the leaves,
To my surprise
Right before my eyes
In a brown prickly rolled-up ball.
Was

a

tiny

hedgehog!

Lisa Parr (11)
Bloomfield Collegiate

My Autumn Scene

I see all my friends arrive
I'm as excited as a pup
I see all my decorations
And my family all dressed up.

I smell the snacks from the kitchen
And the candy apples I made.
I smell the candles burning, as the flames start to fade.

I hear all the trick or treaters singing
And the laughing of my friends.
I feel happy being with my family and enjoy the message
Autumn sends.

Jodi Doherty (12)
Bloomfield Collegiate

My Autumn Scene

The trees and their leaves,
that's what everyone sees,
but I see something special
I see nature and it is beautiful.

Sometimes I stand and wonder
at the enormous chestnut trees,
the smell of toffee apples and
the smell of pumpkin pie.

Golden brown, yellow and red,
the colours are amazing.
The leaves come floating down
a colourful carpet under my feet.

My worries, my cares are gone
when I see this scene.
The beautiful scene of *autumn!*

Melanie Gibson (12)
Bloomfield Collegiate

All I Want

Walking through the distinct odour of decaying bodies,
Looking around at the disaster zone that we live in every day.
Searching for some kind of comfort,
Coughing, coughing, trying to suck in any kind of oxygen
That surrounds me,
Lungs fit to burst from poison in the air.
'Over the top!' they shout.
The cries of the poor individuals who pass over into their new life,
Their souls pierced as easily with the experience of the trenches,
as their bodies are with the sharp bullet from a gun.
All I want is my life back,
My old life,
A new life,
Any life.

Elizabeth Peace (14)
Bloomfield Collegiate

Autumn

Summer has ended,
Pink skies drift slowly.
As my dad rakes up a mountain
Of golden crunchy leaves.
A gentle breeze blows over,
That tranquil swaying mountain.
The quick chirps of singing,
Birds echo down the garden.
The fading smell of flowers,
Hangs in the air like fog.
I place some juicy berries in my mouth
Which are at their freshest.
Brushing past brambles which
Feel like a wasp's sting.

Amanda Watterson (12)
Bloomfield Collegiate

Autumn Time

The leaves are falling like crisp snowflakes,
Mum is making cakes,
Laughter has finally come.
Oh how autumn time is fun.

Collecting conkers, children run,
They shout, as they have fun.
Oh autumn makes me feel so nice,
I wish that it came twice.

Waving through the air on wings like a dove
The smell of autumn, I love.
Cinnamon, ginger and pumpkin pie,
It goes so quickly. But why?

Norah Officer (11)
Bloomfield Collegiate

My Autumn Poem

I open my gateway to autumn and my golden dog
Bounds out
Into the crisp, golden sunshine
And then I hear my mum shout,
'Look, look, there's a fox about!'

See the autumn leaves falling
Their colours all so bright
Lying on the freshly cut grass
Under the big oak tree.
What a lovely sight!

The atmosphere is so soothing
Hear the little birds chirping
A relaxing autumn song,
Sweetening the air
Before the Harvest Fair.

Walking to my granny's
With my family and my dog,
We cut across the corn-cut fields
And find a little frog.
We take it to the river
To make sure it's okay,
We see it hop further and further away.

Nicola Shepherd (11)
Bloomfield Collegiate

Autumn

Oranges, reds, browns and greens,
The chestnut-brown conkers growing through
the multicoloured leaves.
Autumn time is a breeze in the wind,
a tree on the hill,
a golden sun in the sky.
Summer has gone now, we say bye-bye!

Rachel Martin (12)
Bloomfield Collegiate

Autumn

Autumn comes
Crisp and golden,
Summer's gone,
But not forgotten.
Blackberries ripe,
Apples sweet.
Fallen leaves
Under my feet.

Toffee apples,
Pumpkin pie,
Conkers and acorns,
Swallows fly.
Ears of corn
Bales of hay,
Harvest moon,
Shorter days.

Autumn ends
The leaves are gone
Now the winter
Seems so long.

Chloe Lynas (12)
Bloomfield Collegiate

Autumn

I walked along the footpath
And there before my eyes
A multicoloured carpet
Oh what a surprise!

Red, yellow, brown and green,
It was the loveliest sight I'd ever seen.

To look at it was not enough
My feet just wanted to run.
Crunch, crunch, crunch, crunch,
It was so much fun.

Rebecca Lucas (12)
Bloomfield Collegiate

I Am . . .

(Inspired by 'Woman Of The Future' by Cathy Warry)

I am all I see,
My family getting older
Pop stars and celebrities on TV.

I am all I hear,
Angry men tooting car horns,
Alarm clocks going off in the morning.

I am all I feel,
Happy when I'm with friends and family,
Sad when I'm alone.

I am all I taste,
Mum's pasta
And Sunday dinners.

I am all I remember,
My brother being born,
Sleepwalking around the house.

I am all I've been taught,
Don't mix colours in washing,
The times tables.

I am all I think,
What should I do next?
Where should I go?

I am like a go-kart,
But one day I'll slow down and become
The responsible young lady that
I'm supposed to be!

I am the woman of the future.

Lisa Hollywood (13)
Bloomfield Collegiate

I Am . . .

(Inspired by 'Woman Of The Future' by Cathy Warry)

I am all I see,
    The breathtaking view from an
    Aeroplane's window.

I am all I hear,
    Respect your elders.
    Pollution is at an all time high.

I am all I feel,
    Ice cream running down my chin,
    Carpet underneath my toes.

I am all I taste,
    Brussels sprouts at Christmas time,
    Honey slipping down my throat.

I am all I remember,
    My grandad telling me never to smoke,
    Even though he did!

I am all I've been taught,
    Nine nines are eighty-one,
    A noun is a person, place or thing!

I am all I think,
    When will I ever grow up?
    That is so unfair.

I am like a signet,
    But one day I will emerge from childhood
    And become a beautiful swan, because
    I am the woman of the future.

Victoria Scott (13)
Bloomfield Collegiate

I Am . . .

(Inspired by 'Woman Of The Future' by Cathy Warry)

I am all I see,
    The happy smile on my brother's face,
    The rainy weather and dull grey sky.

I am all I hear,
    Girls chatting and giggling in the corridor,
    Children laughing and screaming in the playground.

I am all I feel,
    My teddies on my bed, all cuddly and soft,
    Waves lapping and crashing against my feet.

I am all I taste,
    The sweet and cold taste of delicious banoffee pie,
    The taste of a mouth-watering, greasy Ulster fry!

I am all I remember,
    Running and falling on my face, grazing both my knees,
    Passing swivel hips in trampolining class.

I am all I have been taught,
    Always remember your manners,
    BODMAS in mathematics.

I am all I think,
    Secrets never to be told,
    What clothes shall I wear today?

I am like seeds and this is my packet,
    But one day I will break free
    And grow into a flower because . . .
I am the woman of the future.

Rebekah Robinson (13)
Bloomfield Collegiate

I Am . . .

(Inspired by 'Woman Of The Future' by Cathy Warry)

I am all I see,
>Friends looking happy when the bell rings on a Friday,
>My dog begging for food at the dinner table.

I am all I hear,
>The birds singing in the morning,
>The ticking of the clock in the classrooms.

I am all I feel,
>The warm lick from my dog,
>The smoothness of the piano keys.

I am all I taste,
>Bitter orange juice in my mouth,
>The fresh taste of baked bread.

I am all I remember,
>Falling off my bike and getting stitches,
>Getting my 11+ results.

I am all I've been taught,
>Learning how to spell your French vocabulary,
>Reading up to chapter two in your novels.

I am all I think,
>What will I be when I'm older?
>What would the world be like if Adam and Eve
>had not eaten the fruit?

I am like a bud wanting to grow into a flower,
But one day I'll grow and turn into a kind, beautiful,
clever woman but for now . . .
I'm the girl of the present.

Janet Martin (12)
Bloomfield Collegiate

I Am . . .

(Inspired by 'Woman Of The Future' by Cathy Warry)

I am all I see
When the sun sets on the horizon in the evening,
When the flowers bloom in the summer

I am all I hear
The theme tune of my favourite TV programme
My friend's voice on the phone.

I am all I feel
The warmth of the sun beaming on my skin
And sitting in my car while it's raining.

I am all I taste
Going to the café at the weekend with my friends
And licking an ice cream while walking to the beach.

I am all I remember
Lying in my warm bed on a cold winter's day

I am all I've been taught
Don't talk to strangers
Always tell the truth.

I am all I think
What clothes should I wear?
Do I look okay?

I am like a daffodil sitting in the sun, but one day
I will bloom and be appreciated for what I am.
I am the woman of the future.

Natasha Gunning (13)
Bloomfield Collegiate

I Am . . .

(Inspired by 'Woman Of The Future' by Cathy Warry)

I am all I see,
Specks of dust floating in the sunlight,
Cars rushing round in a craze.

I am all I hear,
Engines revving with power and strength,
The pattering of raindrops on my window sill.

I am all I feel,
The warmth I have in me after hot chocolate,
Snowflakes melting on my tongue.

I am all I taste,
Luxurious chocolates Mum has brought home,
Sticky toffee clasping to my teeth.

I am all I remember,
Drifting to the bottom of the swimming pool,
Newborn puppies, helpless and needy.

I am all I've been taught,
Don't run in the corridors!
Treat others as you would want to be treated.

I am all I think,
Who am I really?
Why do cats miaow?

I am like a dandelion growing amongst the nettles,
But one day I'll bear my seeds and the wind will guide me
In different directions because . . .
I am the woman of the future.

Nicola Black   (13)
Bloomfield Collegiate

I Am . . .

(Inspired by 'Woman Of The Future' by Cathy Warry)

I am all I see
A horse cantering around a field
Trees bashing around in the wind.

I am all I hear
The smashing of a plate
A stone splashing into still waters of a lake.

I am all I feel
The soft muzzle of a foal
Prickly grass beneath my feet.

I am all I taste
Strong chocolate milkshake
Sweet and juicy melon.

I am all I remember
Being lost in the shopping centre
Having an extra large ice cream.

I am all I've been taught
A verb is a 'doing' word
An ostrich is the biggest bird alive.

I am all I think
What will I be when I grow up?
Why is the sky blue?

I am like a spark
But one day I will become a roaring, blazing fire.

I am the woman of the future.

Jennifer McKee (12)
Bloomfield Collegiate

I Am . . .

(Inspired by 'Woman Of The Future' by Cathy Warry)

I am all I see
At Christmas my big family all gathered round the Christmas tree.

I am all I hear
My dreaded alarm clock that wakes me up each morning.

I am all I feel
An ice-cold snowflake that swiftly drops on my face.

I am all I taste
The juicy taste of summer fruits.

I am all I remember
My holiday in the sun, heat glaring on my back.

I am all I have been taught
Don't talk to strangers, say no to drugs.

I am all I think
Will I be allowed out tonight? Homework or TV?

I am like . . .
A dolphin swimming in the sea but one day I will be
Leaping out of the water, not afraid to show what I can do.

I am the woman of the future.

Rebecca Blakley (13)
Bloomfield Collegiate

I Am . . .

(Inspired by 'Woman Of The Future' by Cathy Warry)

I am all I see,
Butterflies, rainbows, war, death and destruction.

I am all I hear,
Singing, music, crying, screaming, bombs and crashes.

I am all I feel,
Warm, secure, loved, happy, cold, wet and afraid.

I am all I taste,
Hot potatoes with melted butter, stale bread and water.

I am all I remember,
Family, friends, outings, holidays, ships and leaving home.

I am all I have been taught,
Love everyone and be their friend,
Get underneath your desk if an earthquake occurs.

I am all I think,
What's for dinner? Where will I go when I die?
Is it alright?

I am like me, myself and I
But I am nothing else
Just what I create for myself
To do and to say.

I am everything I am meant to be.

Jenny Moth (12)
Bloomfield Collegiate

My Autumn Poem

It is time to pack away our summer gear
Because autumn is close, it's oh so near.
It's a beautiful day outside,
The wind is strong and whistling at me,
As if it's telling a secret.

Leaves litter the ground like a multicoloured carpet,
Rusty copper colours of red, yellow, orange and brown
Surrounding me,
As well as the strong oak trees they've fallen from.
My dog stands out as white as snow against
This colourful scene.

I take a deep breath of crisp, fresh air,
It's like being by the sea.
I watch squirrels busy as bees
Store up for hibernation.
Conkers lie on the ground, they are so smooth
To touch and are a rich colour of chestnut brown.

Summer is dead but I'm not sad,
Because autumn really isn't half bad!

Amy Rollins (12)
Bloomfield Collegiate

I Am . . .

(Inspired by 'Woman Of The Future' by Cathy Warry)

I am all I see,
The sun beaming on my face on a beautiful day,
And a butterfly flying around the garden.

I am all I hear,
The bird outside singing in a tree in the morning,
And the wind howling outside on a cool winter's morning,

I am all I feel,
The feeling of thin sand on my feet at the beach,
And the waves hitting my legs.

I am all I taste,
The bitter taste of a lemon,
And the rough feeling of candyfloss sitting on my tongue.

I am all I remember,
The pain in my throat when I had my tonsils out,
And getting my letter, telling me that I'd got into Bloomfield.

I am all I've been taught,
Learning my ABCs in primary school,
And that smoking gives you lung cancer.

I am all I think,
What will I be like later on in life?
Will I get my dream job?

I'm like a fly caught inside a sticky spider's web
Trying to wriggle my way free,
But one day I will get out of the web because
I am the woman of the future.

Jill Moreland (12)
Bloomfield Collegiate

I Am . . .

(Inspired by 'Woman Of The Future' by Cathy Warry)

I am all I see,
Crisp, golden leaves floating in an autumn breeze,
Raindrops, dancing on the road like hundreds of mini ballerinas.

I am all I hear,
The annoying DJ on the radio talking over my favourite song.
Howling dogs at midnight chatting away to each other.

I am all I feel,
The pounding headache coming home from school on a stormy
Monday afternoon.
The terror as you realise that odd sensation on your arm is
indeed, a spider.

I am all I taste,
The minty taste of the world's thinnest Polo mint which finally snaps.
The sour taste of warm Coke that hasn't been put in the fridge.

I am all I remember,
Falling over and scarring my knee at my first attempt at cycling,
And loving Chinese food the first time I tried it.

I am all I've been taught.
Thousand, hundreds, tens and units. Having to learn that,
day after day.
Division, multiplication, addition and subtraction and having to learn
that day after day too.

I am all I think,
Why does popcorn pop?
Where are my socks?

I am like a fish . . .
Trapped in the current of a rushing, raging river.
But one day I'll grow, I'll become a big fish
And some day I'll have a river of my own.

I am the woman of the future.

Victoria Potts (13)
Bloomfield Collegiate

My Autumn Poem

A lovely, crisp afternoon to walk,
The dogs come bounding up.
The wind blows, swiftly and gently,
Leaves swirl *around* and *around*
There aren't very many leaves on the trees
It's as if the path is painted *gold, red* and *orange.*

Back we walk along the leafy path
I hear a rustling noise from a bush
A hedgehog making its nest
A squirrel scurrying up a tree
Look, a squirrel collecting nuts for winter.

Home we head,
We arrive at my house
A lovely smell wafts through the air.
I can almost taste
My mum's gorgeous Hallowe'en apple pie!

Jenna Adamson (11)
Bloomfield Collegiate

The Titanic

Looking through the window
Now I clearly see
The people of the Titanic
Staring back at me.

The people in the lifeboats
I hear their cries and screams
As the great ship Titanic
Sinks slowly into the seas.

I'm glad I'm getting off now
With my family and my friends
But the great ship Titanic
Will haunt me to the end.

Alice Blackstock (11)
Lagan College

Preposition

I lost my preposition
I looked everywhere
I couldn't find it anywhere
So I tried my teddy bear,

I ran up the stairs
Looked at the clock
I couldn't find it there,
Except for a smelly sock.

I went into the garden
Looked behind the shed
Couldn't find it there
So I tried the flower bed,

I went into the kitchen
Looked in a file,
There was my preposition
Lying in a pile.

Mary Brown (11)
Lagan College

Donegal At Night (When It's Not Raining)

Dotted across the sky
Like rhinestones on a dress,
Permanently resembling diamonds
Just taking away your breath.

Forgetting who you are
No need for a name,
The night has magnificent beauty
For once you're glad you came.

The clouds form a backdrop
They're the canvas for your art,
Beneath the stars are river and mountains
You can't even notice, you're falling apart.

Emma Gallen (14)
Lagan College

The Animal Shop

You may think it's strange,
You may think it's queer,
But animals have
A little shop, near!

Animals order objects,
Even from underground
From this little shop
Which adult minds still haven't found.

And the mole
As he passes
Orders some
Sunglasses!

'They're perfect! They're perfect!'
Says the mole, again and again.
'They're different from the other ones,
They don't make me look insane!'

And the giraffe who wanted a three metre scarf,
Just called to say
She wanted patterns of yellow and brown
And she wanted it today!

'It fits! It fits!'
Said the giraffe, excitedly
And she left the shop
But she didn't say it quietly!

The puss who waited patiently,
Wanted some new boots.
She said that she was fed up
And wanted a change in her looks.

'They're big, they're black and they're bulky!
They're just right for me.
There'll be stories written about me and these boots,
I'll make history!'

The reason adults can't find
This wonderful creation,
Well the reason's simple you see
They have no imagination!

Santa Claus and the Easter Bunny
All they can do is smile,
They will exist, no matter what
In the innocence of a child.

So let them be kids, run wild and free,
Before the teen 'abomination'
And remember that the most wonderful things
Come from children's imaginations.

Carla McGaharan (12)
Lagan College

The Mirror

All this time is where I stay
When full of love but there's no way
Everything in this world
Come again without a word
With the blue sky every day
The mountains come but never stay
Through the snowy hills, I'll find the path
That will lead me to the only way
What will become of me?
The only soul left to die
From everyone I know, it's the only thing left
The way in which I will become forever
When death comes to all of us
It will never be the way it was
As what to see in the windowpane
Comes along every day
I will see you come but once again
One day there is a hope
But when it is I don't know
When the rattles come along all day
And when you can't ever get free
I'll see you for evermore
Happiness comes but once in a while
And soon enough I can meet you there
With my reflection in the mirror.

Natalie Smyth (14)
Lagan College

A Day In The Life Of . . .

Round and round and round
I go, it makes me rather dizzy,
The only friend I have down here
Copies me and looks like he's in a tizzy.

My name's Tarzan and no
I don't swing from trees,
I swim about in a bowl all day
And life is such a breeze.

Except when this furry thing comes,
The owner calls it a cat,
It tries to jump inside my bowl,
But I'm having none of that.

Twice a day they give me food
They change me twice a week,
All in all I can't complain
Life is rather sweet.

Oh yeah and by the way
In case you haven't guessed it,
I'm a fish and very rich
Be careful, I'm made of gold!

Kaya Carville (11)
Lagan College

A Weird Hallowe'en Dream

H airy
A nd scary
L ooming in the dark
L ights flicker in the park.
O h, it's just a firework
W here your worst fears lurk
E nter into your worst nightmare
E ventually it rips and tears, I
N oticed in my creepy Hallowe'en dream - Wahoo!

Finn MacMillan (11)
Lagan College

Autumn

Dead leaves fallen, their dry crunch
Temporarily muffled by the rain.
Rain that has been waiting months
To comfort its natural soulmate.

Clouds start to loom, infinite shades of grey
Shade the ground from the tired sun.
Elsewhere, where the sun is low but clear,
Gnat clouds swarm over young rivers
Orange in the evening light.

The trees are all bare, ready to hibernate with the sun,
While at the same time, squirrels are preparing for their
Own hibernation
Scampering around the damp moss gathering
Provisions for the harsh winter to come.
This is autumn.

Myles McCormack (14)
Lagan College

Autumn

Autumn's a wonderful season as the weather
Begins to change,
The golden brown leaves dry up and fall,
Twisting and turning to the ground.
The gentle sun plumps and ripens the fruit
Ready to be harvested,
The gossamer webs sparkle from the dew
Of the morning,
The climate starts to change and brings
A chill to the air.
The squirrels scurry from the trees in a hurry
To collect food for the coming winter.
Heavy brown pine cones drop from the trees,
The light begins to fade as the nights get longer
And soon enough autumn turns into winter.

Nicola McColgan (14)
Lagan College

The Fairground

Would you believe what I have found?
Would you believe how much my life is just like
The fairground?

My life goes up and it goes down, that's what I've found,
My life is just like a roller coaster
At the fairground.

In my life people come in and go, when for them it's sound,
Just like all the rides
At the fairground.

People only come near me when they see fun abound,
Just like all the visitors who enjoy themselves
At the fairground.

Still my life goes round and round,
Just like the Ferris wheel
At the fairground.

I must live a life where my hands are bound,
Just like the bars, just like
The fairground.

Would you believe what I have found?
Would you believe how much my life is
Just like the fairground?

Ryan Huddleston (15)
Lagan College

The Garden At 6am

Flowers swaying in the breeze,
With their long stems.
Paper petals flying through the clouds,
Beautiful colours on every side,
As I walk through the garden at 6am.

Peter Luke Woods (11)
Lagan College

Autumn

While the low sun beams down,
Silver spiderwebs start to glitter.
The chilly wind whistles softly,
While golden, crunchy leaves flutter.
The chimney tops are surrounded by
The smell of warm soup.
Heavy rain slides down windows,
Conkers fall to the ground from trees,
As it starts to get darker,
The clocks are turned back.
Fireworks fly out of nowhere
Bursting out bright rainbow colours
And when you walk through the door
The warm fire crackles gently.

Hollie Corbin (14)
Lagan College

My Best Friend

My best friend is Mary,
For eleven years I've told her all my secrets
And I can trust her not to breathe a word.
She shares my special times,
And comforts me when I'm sad.
She's loyal and faithful.
Mary is my holiday companion,
And beside me in a thousand adventures.
Sailing around the world,
From frozen Poles to exotic lands.
My twin?
No, my special teddy!

Mairi Skinner (11)
Lagan College

Rats

I used to live in a country house
That was really, really, really nice,
The only thing wrong with the house was
It was overrun by a family of mice.

I went out the next day to buy some cats
'Cause maybe it wasn't mice but rats!
The thought of rats is horrid to me
I'm scared of rats, you see!

I locked myself up in the dorm
And let the cats out in the morn,
I opened the door to look out and see
There were three black rats looking up at me.
My cats were standing very near,
Why did you bring them in, oh dear!

My brother came in and scooped them up
And put them in the garden tub.
I hope that's the last I'll see
Of those horrible rats that so scare me.

Shannon Stewart (12)
Lagan College

Oak Tree

Oak tree, oak tree,
Way up high, way up high in the sky
Every day as I see
I see you watching over me.

Oak tree, oak tree
In the sky
In the sky, way up high
With your branches blowing wild
I always want to look outside.

Andrew Harper (12)
Lagan College

With No Home

Here I stand
All alone
By myself
And with no home.

Days go by
People pass
No one cares
That's me - third class!

Although I try,
And try again
No one cares
Not one friend.

My name shall stay
And always will,
Engraved in stone
Still, with no home.

Stephanie Fleck (13)
Lagan College

Down

Trapped in a room where nobody knows,
quiet and peaceful.
Don't wanna blow my nose
trying to keep my cool.
I really don't wanna be a fool,
My life ain't worth living,
All alone.

Down in the dumps, scared and alone,
All I'm doing is moan
moan
moan!

Zoë Latimer (11)
Lagan College

Lagan College

Lagan College is so much fun
Different classes to be done
Lots of homework, not much fun
Maths has too many sums
Spanish is my favourite one
History can be the boring one.

Different subjects every hour
PE we run too far,
IT uses up the power,
Music I hope to play quieter
I could end up being a rock star.
Heaven on Earth it is for me,
Drama, I'd rather drink some tea.
It's come to the end; one thing to say
Lagan College is the one for me!

Gavin McKee (12)
Lagan College

Autumn

Autumn resembles a poem; it's fresh, new and sometimes
complicated,
Autumn, when you stand in the middle of a park surrounded by trees,
You close your eyes and you can hear the newly fallen leaves
swirling frantically at your feet.
The smells of autumn are so obvious, like an icy breeze or the smell
of burning wood.
The morning dew is drying out and the fields are ready to harvest.
Mists suspended at my feet and the flowers wasting slowly away.
The poppies on the ground and the conkers high in the trees,
The darker nights gradually rolling in, ready for the harvest moon
to begin.
Animals gathering food for hibernation and the birds migrating south,
All of these play a part in autumn.

Amber Kynes (14)
Lagan College

A Fire Is . . .

A burst of temper,
 A destructive force,
  A giant fiery furnace
   Fiercely explosive,
    Raging flames,
     A river of fire.
Fire of God,
 Unstoppable tongues,
  Blood rushing,
   Risking life,
    A lion's mane,
     Tiger stripes
Sparks that lick the surface,
 Burning greatly,
  Shooting stars,
   Vivid imagination,
    Darting fish,
     Tail lights through a wet windscreen.
Pink flamingos,
 Curtains blowing in the wind,
  A friend, a foe,
   Going out,
    Gone out!

Abigail Cahoon (15)
Lagan College

New Beginnings

Down the empty road I can see
A whole new life in front of me;
Back there is the life I left behind
For a new life only I can find;
Though my old life will be hard to forget,
The new life will have its bit.
In this new chapter of my life -
New beginnings.

Lauren Crowe (14)
Methodist College

No Time

They're gone now, I have some time
To clean my wounds and clear my head.
The pain throbs but fear is worse,
A dam of sorrow, sure to burst.

But now they're back, I have no time
To hide away and try to shield myself,
A silent fist, the silent screams,
The silent shatter of a thousand dreams.

Since they've been back, all the time.
Abuse rains down as tears stream my face,
Forever searching for a glimmer of hope,
But this life is agony, I just can't cope.

Others are back but they have no time,
Can't they see the pain I'm in?
They have the key to the door of my prison,
But they have no time to stop and listen.

They're gone now, I have the time
To look back at the misery of each day
And realise they just don't care
And I'll never be free from this nightmare.

Aimée Muirhead (13)
Methodist College

The Polar Bear

Her fur was as soft as feathers,
White snow surrounded her.
She was hard to see at first,
As she was as white as the snow around her.
The top of the highest mountain
Is where I saw her last,
A fish wriggling in her grasp.
Unlike me she looked warm,
And all of a sudden came the storm,
Then she went back to her baby born.

Emma Kirk (12)
Methodist College

The Last Photo

I remember that moment, only one year ago,
When we stood in the garden with smiles on our faces.
I remember what you smelt like, I remember that you laughed,
Whilst we stood in the garden with smiles on our faces.
I remember your touch, your warm hands around me,
Standing in that garden with smiles on our faces.

I remember the pain that tore through my heart
When I stood by that bed with a smile on my face.
I remember the fear that I saw in your eyes,
Whilst I stood by that bed with a smile on my face.
I remember that I kissed you, before I left you alone,
Lying in that bed with a smile on your face.

I remember the moment when my world collapsed,
As I read those words with tears in my eyes.
I remember my dad as he clung to my hand,
Whilst we sat there together with tears in our eyes.
I remember watching the coffin disappear,
Standing in the church with little drops of heartbreak
rolling down my cheeks.

I remember that day in the garden
When you stood beside me with a smile on your face.
I remember every day how happy you were
Whilst you stood beside me with a smile on your face.
I remember you and tears fill my eyes again,
I wish you were still standing beside me now.

Rachael Barnes (15)
Methodist College

Panther

The panther is as black as the night,
It never appears in daylight.
Its claws are like steel,
It looks for a meal,
So you'd better look out for its bite!

Rory McKenna (12)
Methodist College

Says The Child To The Neighbour

No, I can't come out to play,
I just made plans to run away.
Yes, I know I'm only four,
But I don't matter anymore.
There's a baby here today.

Mum invited the family over,
Cooing at my baby brother.
I can do much more than he,
Lots of presents, none for me,
I'm not worth the bother.

Mum and Daddy don't want me,
That's why he was born, you see.
I must be getting far too old,
I'm a big girl now, so I'm told.
There's no room here for me.

So as I said, all I can do
Is run away to somewhere new.
Where I'm going, I don't know,
About as far as I can go . . .
. . . Can I please stay with you?

Giulia Giordano (14)
Methodist College

The Puma

A pair of emerald eyes shine in the dark,
Glowing as bright as green flames spark.

A sleek coat of fur so black
Moves stealthily on the forest track.

Low to the ground hunting its prey,
The puma sniffs and silently turns away.

Invisible to all in the darkest shadows of the trees,
The creatures of the jungle listen and freeze.

Gawain Hill (12)
Methodist College

Unfinishing Dream And A Brown Paper Parcelled Box

Bare, blank, blue walls
  Full of cluster and clutter,
A map of the world,
And a long, brooding mirror.

A box stands alone
  With the rest of my desk,
It seems to stand out,
As if it were blessed.

This box intrigues me
  In a curious sort of way,
It has no label,
Did it arrive here this day?

I ponder a while
  And search through my thoughts,
I pull at the string,
It feels harsh, soft, white and taut.

Oh how I wish I could open that box and
  Discover for myself the treasures inside . . .

Sean Esmonde (15)
Methodist College

Pounce!

Its eyes are as bright as fire,
They stare straight into the night.

Its body is lying as low as it can be,
It's poising for a fight.

Its claws are sharper than ten knives,
Coloured a pearly white.

It moves as quickly as lightning,
Its prey is out like a light.

Kate Robinson (12)
Methodist College

The Lion

The lion stalks his prey
Like a snail moving.
His fur camouflages him
As if he is disappearing.

He looks up like
He is looking at a skyscraper.
He puts power into his knees
Like he is blowing.

He jumps
Up high
And sinks his jaw into
His victim like a snake.

He drags his prize
When he kills it,
And brings it home
As if he is going to be congratulated.

Shajeth Srigengan (11)
Methodist College

The Eagles' Hunt

Flying through the air so swift,
Over the mountain and snowdrift.
Through the canyons tall and wide,
Now we're at the other side . . .

The air is pure, the water sweet,
This is where we like to meet.
We soar together from far away,
We hunt like leopards, day after day.

Then far below, behind a tree,
The prey is spotted, a little monkey.
I dive straight down, but he is too quick,
And all I manage is a little nick.

Michael McCrea (11)
Methodist College

Mmmm . . .

Squishy, sugary, full of jam
Eat it quick, as fast as you can.
Don't lick your lips, come on you can do it
Mmmm . . . bite it, swallow when you chew it!

Smooth, creamy, yum, yum, yum,
Melt in your mouth, going in your tum.
Eat as much as you want or as much as you dare,
White, dark or milk chocolate, I don't care!

Cold, soft, from the freezer,
Just one spoonful, a little teaser,
No, a bowlful, oh just a lot
Ice cream, I want it, vanilla or not!

Green, crunchy, bits of red,
Leave it on the plate, no force it down instead.
I don't really want it, tastes like dirt,
If I don't eat salad, I don't get desert!

Christina Bennington (12)
Methodist College

The Owl

The owl was as silent as the darkest of nights.
She perched in the shadows of the woods, waiting.

The shrew scampered like a leaf in the wind,
Crackling the twigs that lay under his feet.

She flew as swiftly as a bullet, her talons curling
Around her small and furry food.

He lay on the branch like the soldier
Who had been hit by the bullet, dead.

Amy Kirk-Smith (11)
Methodist College

Personified

I look out and see the early morning sunrise,
It's like a roaring fire being woken up.
Hundreds of different colours soar across the sky
As the day comes to life.

The rain leaves droplets of water everywhere,
Making everything crisp go soggy and damp.
Anything lush, dry and clean
Clings to life as the rain washes over it.

The wind calls out in gusts of cold air,
Rampaging through the forests and trees.
The icy cold feeling as it passes over you,
As if that breath was its last.

The snow blankets everything in its path,
Leaving a layer of secrets underneath.
The harsh, white glow makes everything seem hazy
As the icy bite snaps at your touch.

Each one has its own life,
Just as it has its own name.
Whether it be wind or rain,
Or snow or sun,
They all live just like beings,
But they are different.
They are personified.

Priyanka Nayar
Methodist College

How To Make An Arctic Fox

He needs . . .
Furry skin, to glisten like the snow he walks on,
A long tail to stick up like a snow-covered pine tree,
Short stubby legs to look as though he is on tree stumps,
A white face, with a small grey nose, shining like a marble
And his long white hairs should stand like frosty grass.

Mark Osborne (11)
Methodist College

From My Bedroom Window

From my bedroom window, I can see wet clothes hanging on the line,
The battered blue ball in the neighbour's garden that I know was
once mine.
I see the giggly girl, playing in her ancient shed,
And her older brother staggering home from a night out,
Now so eager to get to bed.

From my bedroom window, I can see our twisting street,
The gentle geriatric cat, Dino, unsteady on his feet,
I see furry pines that have recently had a trim,
And the splash of tiny, coloured blue tits,
As in the deep puddles they swim.

From my bedroom window, I can see cows grazing in fields far away,
Dotted between them, the occasional pony, nibbling on some hay.
I see past my little street and there is nothing but countryside.
A tractor stutters and coughs along a dusty track,
Before its sickly engine, at last, gives up and dies.

As night draws in, street lamps hurriedly flicker on,
Neighbours begin to clamber up the stairs and won't wake till dawn,
A sound suddenly pierces the silent air as a car begins to beep,
And my mum drags the heavy curtains closed,
And yells, 'It's time to go to sleep!'

Sonia Hill (16)
Methodist College

How To Make A Cheetah

He needs . . .
His fierce face like the face of a monster,
His strong and fast legs, which could outrun the engine of a Ferrari,
His amazing patterns which are unending, like a long and
unwinding maze,
His whole body, which is so fit and built for speed and his stamina
which goes on like the battery of a car.

Daniel Culbert (12)
Methodist College

Out The Window

I look out the window,
All there is is trees and grass,
Green and brown.
But then I look closer,
Off to the left.
In the bushes I see a frog,
Sometimes I look out and
The garden is bare,
But what I realise is life carries on out there,
It's not affected by the seasons,
Just keeps going on and on.
As the sun sets, I look out the window again,
The colours have grown deeper,
And in the distance I imagine
Is a solitary home
Perched on the mountain tops.

Jonathan Geoghegan (16)
Methodist College

Wild Girl

Listening to the wild girl cry out in the night,
Her purpose is lethal and spreads like a blight.
How many? I wonder. I do not know
If she's done this before or is it a show.
I listen, I listen but I don't want to hear,
That's when I realise she's getting near.
I'm smothering, drowning in her grasp,
It's killing me, I'm dying, how long will this last?
The end is soon, I'm feeling bare,
I break away and she's still there.
Running on, got to get away,
I don't know how I could ever stay.
I'm nothing now, not even a ghost,
But that's what she wanted, wanted the most.

Jane Burrell (15)
Methodist College

The View From The Window

Through the glistening trees, the lone crow flies,
On an ever lowering arc o'er frostbitten ground.
His path ever monitored by the cunning fox
Who sits in his ditch, waiting to pounce.

The peace is shattered by the dog
Barking at the low flying helicopter.
An endless onward drone goes on and on,
Melting my head like butter on my toast.

The melodic hum as the water fills the pond
Has been eradicated by the bitterly cold wind.
The ice particles glisten as the early morning sun
Shines on its low wintry path.

In the distant fields the cattle stampede,
I wonder why they are not tucked up in the shed.
Nevertheless, the lone crow calls out its last desperate cry.
The cunning fox returns to its lair.

Graeme Nesbitt (16)
Methodist College

A View From A Window (In New York)

Yellow cabs and neon signs,
Fast food outlets where one dines,
Towering buildings stretch so tall,
A feeling of being extremely small.
Bustling people with places to go,
Does this city ever slow?
But in the distance, a stark contrast,
A dark memory from the past.
An eerie silence, an empty space,
A tragic incident has marred this place.

Jenny Collins (16)
Methodist College

Autumnal Splendour

Outside my window
I see . .
Bare arms silhouetted against
An azure blue sky,
Rich and vibrant autumnal colours
Bursting into flames,
Red,
    Gold,
        Orange,
            Yellow,
Birdless wings dancing like flames
Twisting and turning
Gently cascade
                To the soft carpet below.

Hasini Bolleddula (15)
Methodist College

Rio

The city stretches before me,
I can see everything.
The skyscrapers rising into the sky,
And the businessmen walking.

But behind the façade.
The favelas lie,
Hundreds of shacks grouped together,
The children running, not joyfully,
But running in fear.

In the distance, upon the horizon,
Jesus Christ stands watching
And with that image,
I merely close my window.

Peter Campbell (15)
Methodist College

The Penguin

Icy winds blow,
Freezing harsh winds
Although the cold is beautiful
It is deadly.

It waddles awkwardly
Like a pendulum,
As it rocks
From one foot to the other
Hurrying unsuccessfully.

It gets to the brink
It will soon be freed
From the tempest
Of the Polar wastes.

Slowly
It slides over the last snowdrift
Like a toboggan
Only smoother.

It dives
Taking everything around it by surprise
Like an arrow
Plumed with black and white.

For it,
It must be paradise,
To be back in its own element,
Where it is beautiful,
Not awkward.

Cosima Stewart (11)
Methodist College

Memory

On the other side of the glass, the sea stretches out
Like a blue blanket dotted with white stitching.
Waves crashing.

A magpie and his mate chase each other over the grass
Scuttling to and fro, they peck at worms.
Two for joy.

Not a cloud in the sky, the setting summer sun
Creates a hazy horizon in the distance
Miles away.

The white-tipped waves break freely on the shore,
An old man and his granddaughter step cautiously over the stones
Hand in hand.

He scoops her onto his shoulders and carries her up to the road,
Looking to the left, then right, they cross together,
Two for joy.

The figures vanish as if from a dream,
The picture fades, the memory never will.
Two years pass,
Two for joy.

Hannah Lynn (16)
Methodist College

Parrots

Parrots are beautiful and elegant birds.
They have eyes which are shiny and beady, like marbles.
Their feathers are soft and fine like velvet.
They are bright and colourful like a rainbow.
They eat nuts and fruits.
They have beaks which are hard and strong like coconuts.
They also have a point in the tip of their beaks
which is as sharp as a needle.

Iswarya Kalyan (11)
Methodist College

The Chinese Fireball (Dragon)

He flies through the air like fire
Being shot straight into the sky.
He sounds like a booming firework
When he lets out his loudest cry.

A god in control of the demons,
A demon in charge of the gods.
His skin made of solid steel metal,
His bones made of iron rods.

A shadow dwelling in the darkness,
A devil with red glowing eyes.
Anyone who is brave enough to fight him,
Can be sure of their demise.

Power to him is no stranger,
Death to him is a friend.
Warrior above all of the armies,
The ruler of Earth till the end.

Dean Johnson (12)
Methodist College

The View

A huge cherry blossom tree leans over the garden like an old friend.
To the left, the smoke from the chimneys of the nearby houses makes
Them look warm and lived in.
I look out over the rooftops towards the city centre,
The lights on top of the yellow cranes sparkle like stars in the
Summer evening.
The summer rain begins to fall, making a huge pitter-patter
On my skylight.
That is the noise that sometimes wakes me up at night,
With the water pouring in and soaking my carpet.
I close the window and turn my back on that silent, suburban view.

Ciara Mulvenna (15)
Methodist College

A Wet Sunday

Obscured by trees a golf course lies,
Dotted by specks of white,
Drowning in the rain.
A lonely church against the sky,
Its members hurrying inside to escape
God's nemesis.
The birds, which sing their lullabies
And always decorate the skies,
Are nowhere to be seen.
Our tree stands resolute against the wind,
Naked and bare,
But beautiful.
In the distance, a sunbeam pierces the clouds,
Bringing a dawn of hope for
This lifeless day.

Matthew Sayers (16)
Methodist College

The Tiger

Piercing eyes of luminous green,
Black striped back that can barely be seen.
Low in the grass or the branches of trees
He waits patiently till his prey he sees.

He prowls around like a stealthy thief,
Through the jungle not disturbing a leaf.
His roar can be heard for miles around,
Other creatures startle at the sound.

A carnivorous beast, he hunts to eat.
Dagger teeth ripping flesh and meat.
Stay well clear he can smell your fear.
He'll stalk and pounce if you venture near.

Peter Logan (12)
Methodist College

The House On Top Of The Hill

Through the smallest of gaps,
Between two facing suburban houses,
The rolling hills of the countryside are tantalizingly visible.
Small houses scattered between clusters of tall evergreen trees,
A single carriageway carrying people through their monotonous
daily routines.

But on top of the hill stands one of the grandest houses in Belfast,
Made of grey, solid stone, towering three storeys high,
It stands proud on top of the hill looking down on the
surrounding countryside
Imposing the suburban complex from which I admire.

It is the middle of winter and my gaze begins to wander left,
Immediately I lose sight of the hills,
All that is visible is the red brick of the facing house,
The snow-capped gutters around the roof
And the sparkling icicles hanging from the unused basketball hoop.

The dark evenings have set in,
And the hill is set alight by the street lights on the carriageway,
And illuminated house windows spread over the hill,
Like sparkling yellow beacons calling me to them.

Even on the coldest of winter evenings,
The faintest outline of children playing on the frost-encrusted sloping
lawn are barely visible,
And it makes me wonder once more
What life would be like in the house
On the top of the hill.

Neil Campbell (16)
Methodist College

My Old Best Friend

As I lay in the deep down ditch
All alone, cut and bruised
Slowly I drifted off to sleep, leaving all the pain behind.

I was in pain and couldn't escape,
How did I get this way?

I went for a walk with someone I thought was my friend
We walked to a cliff and my life disappeared.

I was in pain and couldn't escape,
How did I get this way?

I woke up that morning and met my friend for lunch that day,
We had a good chat and a really nice time
But how did it all go so wrong?

I was in pain and couldn't escape,
How did I get this way?

She was my best friend, from years ago
Well, that is what I thought.
Was I wrong?
Yes I was.
No friend would end your life.

Shannon Ferguson (12)
Methodist College

How To Make A Dragon

He needs . . .
Huge, glistening, yellow eyes, like pools of molten sulphur,
Teeth that shine like a bright, full moon,
Huge wings that block the sun like big, black rain clouds,
Claws sharp like shards of broken glass,
Scales tough like a huge, rough suit of armour,
Body looming like a vast mountain,
Breath scorching like the sun ablaze,
Tail like a huge fork of deadly lightning.

William Albiston (12)
Methodist College

The Banana Skin

(Inspired by 'Fishbones Dreaming' by Matthew Sweeney)

I lay at the bottom of a garden,
In a smelly compost heap,
With other peelings around me,
I slowly drifted off to sleep.

*I didn't like to be that way,
I'd rather have been somewhere else.*

Back to when I was on a plate,
Mushed up into a pulp,
Two big round eyes staring at me.
I felt like shouting, 'Help!'

*I didn't like to be that way,
I'd rather have been somewhere else.*

Back when I was in a fruit bowl,
With apples, oranges and pears,
I was happy with my family,
And space we used to share.

*I didn't like to be that way,
I'd rather have been somewhere else.*

Back to when I was on a shelf,
People passing by,
Then when someone picked me up,
I thought I was going to die.

*I didn't like to be that way,
I'd rather have been somewhere else.*

Back to when I was sunbathing,
Stuck to the branch of a tree,
That was the life,
When I was as happy as could be.

That was the way I liked to be.

Jordan McCulla (12)
Methodist College

The Parrot

The parrot stares out of his cage at a picture of the rainforest.
He dreams of life back in the wild.
He dreams of flying over the green forest canopy,
Like a green carpet beneath him with blue skies above.
He dreams of showing his colours which are as bright as a rainbow.

He dreams of great trees and rivers.
He dreams of scurrying monkeys,
Of flocks of noisy parrots,
Of tropical flowers and fruits and seeds.

Pulled back from his dream
By his owner's call,
'Who's a pretty boy, then?
Who's a pretty boy?'

James Rooney (11)
Methodist College

Holidays

Sun, sand, deep blue sea,
That is where I'd love to be.

Eating an ice cream, swimming in a pool,
Not locked up in boring old school.

Hot, bright, blazing sun,
Holidays are so much fun.

But I'm back home, stuck in class,
What a load of sassafras.

Sun, sand, deep blue sea,
That is where I'd love to be.

Rose McNeill (12)
Methodist College

Skeleton On The Seabed

(Inspired by 'Fishbones Dreaming' by Matthew Sweeney)

Bones lay on the seabed.
A sword was at their side and a black eyepatch
Was covering an empty socket.
Soon they would be lost in a pile of seaweed.

He didn't like to be this way.
He dreamt back to an olden day.

Back to when he was struggling for breath.
Waves were tossing him to and fro.
He was pulled under the water by the storm
And he sunk to the bottom of the sea.

He didn't like to be this way.
He dreamt back to an olden day.

Back to when his ship capsized
In a dark, stormy night.
He slid along the soaking deck
And was thrown overboard.

He didn't like to be this way.
He dreamt back to an olden day.

Back to when there were sunny skies.
He was a pirate with the wind in his hair
And a trusty crew was at his side.
He was known as the king of the sea.

This was where he wanted to stay,
Where the sun shone throughout the day.

Jonnie Hunter (12)
Methodist College

Rhyme Or Reason

Shall I compare thee to a summer's day?
I will, provided I get some good pay.
Come on, it's worth it - I'll give you my time,
And unlike old Shakespeare, I'll make a good rhyme!

For his most famous poem was a sonnet, you see
Line two rhymed with four, and line one rhymed with three.
This went on in a very repetitive way,
With all sorts of things, all too complex to say!

Until after line eight, when the subject did change,
To stuff like 'growing lines', it was all rather strange.
But my poem is different, it of course, will be great,
If my money comes in at a good steady rate!

For if it does not, I am saddened to say,
I'll not have the chance to beat old Will today!

David Johnston (12)
Methodist College

Phoenix

At once it arose from the ashes of death
Its blazing wings like the sun's flames.

It radiated heat like a volcano,
A golden, red and orange plume,
It carried like the flag of its country.

Never in my life have I seen such a thing,
I never expect I shall see one again,
This proud creature so gracious and smooth
But while I was watching a strange thing happened . . .

This wonderful bird, like nothing I have ever seen dropped.
It lay on the snowy peak, dead and cold but then once again
The flames erupted and once more it arose from the ashes of death.

Chris Curry (11)
Methodist College

My Granda

(Dedicated to Henry James Kernaghan McCammond - 1930-2004)

My granda, he's watched over me since I was just a tyke,
He taught me how to read and write and even ride my bike.
He taught me how to lace my shoes and how to do my tie,
He taught me not to cheat or steal and above all not to lie.

My granda was a learned man, he taught me all he knew,
About the world, mathematics, English, science, history too.
My granda, he loved music and he listened to the best,
Sammy Davis, Frank Sinatra, Matt and Deano and the rest.

My granda loved solving problems, for everything he had a way,
And he would always have an answer, even if it took all day.
My granda, he looked after his clothes, yes he was always neat,
With trousers creased and shirts all pressed, polished shoes
on his feet.

My granda loved his wee red car, he'd drive me anywhere,
I'd say, 'I'll walk round home myself,' and he'd say, 'Don't you dare.'
My granda enjoyed a good old laugh, he'd always keep me going,
And even though we messed around, our love would keep on growing.

He always collected me from school, didn't mind having to
wait a while,
And when I jumped into the car, I was greeted with a great, big smile.
Sometimes he and I would go for walks, and just simply have a chat,
I'd tell him all my secrets and we'd talk about this and that.

From him I learnt my manners and not to put myself in harm,
From him I learnt everything, some wisdom but especially my charm.
My granda was a gentleman, he had a heart of solid gold,
But when he raised his eyebrow up, you knew that you'd been told.

My granda made me who I am, who's standing here today,
And now he's gone and left me here so sad and in dismay.
You see my granda became quite ill, and I thought he was
on the mend,
But now nothing can comfort me, because I've lost my best friend.

I've lost a good friend once before, his name was Uncle Jim,
And now my granda's up in Heaven, having a great time with him.

Harry McCammond (16)
Methodist College

Midnight Panther

The moon shines bright
On this still, quiet night.
Nothing moves, all is still,
Except one creature, out to kill.
His sleek shining coat glistens in the night,
Like a still, calm lake reflecting the light.
He creeps along on all four paws,
Like velvet pads with blades for claws.
He cracks no twigs and crunches no bark,
But his blazing eyes gleam in the dark.
His jaw's slightly open in a menacing way,
Revealing huge teeth that tear apart prey.
Then his ears start to twitch and he listens then stops.
His tail gives a swish then suddenly drops.
He crouches down low without a sound,
Then suddenly leaps with one silent bound.

Cathryn Abernethy (12)
Methodist College

How To Make A Labrador Puppy

Body lean and muscular,
With a shiny coat inky-black like the midnight sky.

Paws soft as velvet,
Nails razor-sharp.

Eyes staring like chocolate Maltesers,
Nose as black as coal.

Teeth white like icing glistening on a cake.
Fangs like jagged icicles, hanging from cavernous jaws, like
Stalactites.

Tail slashing like a whip.

Grace Scott (12)
Methodist College

Save The Dolphin

Graceful as a ballet dancer,
Skimming through the waves.
Diving deep as a deep-sea diver,
Exploring forgotten caves.

Playful as a puppy dog,
Swimming, having fun.
Fast as a shooting star,
Racing 'til the day is done.

Endangered as a koala bear,
Almost disappeared forever.
It's not their fault (and we know it)
Dolphins are so kind and clever.

So don't leave your rubbish in the sea,
Use a different fishing net.
We're destroying our world, bit by bit.
What kind of example is that to set?

Clare Madden (12)
Methodist College

My Animal Poem!

A dog . . .
As good as gold.
Short legs that run as fast as an athlete.
When he is scared he whimpers like a baby.
Skin as fluffy and furry as a teddy bear.
Teeth as strong as stone
And a tail that wags when he is happy.
He is as loyal as a friend.

Beth McMullan (11)
Methodist College

Skeleton

My skeleton lay at the bottom of the seabed
I had no organs and I had no head.

I tried to think what I was before
I was a human drifting from the shore.

Before that I was on the beach asleep
And I was laying in a big fat heap.

Before that I was driving to the bay
Hoping to catch some red-hot rays.

Before that I was getting in the car
Knowing that the drive would take an hour.

Before that I was getting dressed
Making sure I looked my best.

Before that I was in my bed
Never thinking that I would soon be dead.

Sam Graham (12)
Methodist College

Fox

A strange animal comes out at night.
It searches for its prey, its eyes alight.
It creeps through a field making no more noise
than a mouse.
It creeps through fields past farms and a house.
It finds its prey and pounces upon it.
It was a poor little rabbit that had fallen by it.
It makes its way back to its den.
Thinking about tomorrow night, a rabbit or a hen?

Bethany Bleakley (11)
Methodist College

Billy Bird

Billy Bird is his name
Talking and singing is his game.
He talks and chirps all day long
And finishes the day with a song.
Out of his cage he flies about
To get him back you have to shout,
'Get back in your cage you silly bird
Or we'll have to have a serious word.'
Locked up for the night
Out of mind and out of sight.

Stephanie Donald (12)
Methodist College

The Polar Bear

Walking across the ice,
Fur as white as the clouds,
Trying to catch a meal
With my claws as sharp as razors.

I plunge my paw into the ocean
Fast as a shooting star.
I spear a juicy seal
And happily settle down to eat.

Katie Kelly (11)
Methodist College

My Poem About A Cat

She stared hard at me,
Eyes as sparkling and as green as emeralds,
Fur as black as night and as soft as velvet,
Her claws as sharp as knives gripping hard
to the fence,
Teeth shining as white as snow.

Celia Ross (11)
Methodist College

Think Froggy Think

(Inspired by 'Fishbones Dreaming' by Matthew Sweeney)

Froggy could feel himself sliding along.
Down through the snake's stomach.
Soon he was a goner.

He didn't like to be this way.
He shut his eyes and tried to think back.

Back to when he was hopping,
Jump, jump the snake gaining on him.
He couldn't keep it up.

He didn't like to be this way.
He shut his eyes and tried to think back.

Back to when he was clinging to a leaf.
He heard something coming.
He was scared, very scared.

He didn't like to be this way.
He shut his eyes and tried to think back.

Back to when he was squirming.
A tadpole in a big puddle
Vulnerable to any passing creature.

He didn't like to be this way.
He shut his eyes and tried to think back.

Back to when he was cuddled up
Inside his jelly
Surrounded by his brothers and sisters.

He liked to be this way
He thought hard to try and stay there.

Debbie Neely (12)
Methodist College

The Car

(Inspired by 'Fishbones Dreaming' by Matthew Sweeney)

The car lay there in the scrap heap,
Amongst the trucks and discarded sheds.
Crippled beyond recognition,
Waiting to be ripped to shreds.

He remembers sitting on the recovery lorry,
Feeling the shudder of its engine.
Hearing his shaken driver mumbling sorry.
Seeing nothing through his cracked vision.

It was raining heavily on the track,
He quickly took a slippery chicane.
Suddenly there was an almighty crack,
And his body was wracked with pain.

Parked in the showroom for weeks and days,
Covered in greasy fingermarks,
Waiting for someone who pays.
Occasionally demonstrating skid parks.

Rolling off the production line,
All shiny, sparkly and new.
Ready to start speeding away,
Leaving a trail of blue.

Alex Maxwell (13)
Methodist College

The Komodo Dragon

She needs . . .
To have eyes that shine like gold in the night.
A body that is like a fallen tree trunk
And legs that are like an athlete's, always ready to run at speed.
She also needs a tail as long as a snake and as strong as an ox.
Last but not least, her mouth is like a black hole with teeth like rocks
Sharpened to a point, ready to snap up anything that enters.

Ryan Annett (11)
Methodist College

The Skeleton

(Inspired by 'Fishbones Dreaming' by Matthew Sweeney)

He lay there on the seabed
All the crabs washed up as well
He couldn't move, he couldn't talk
No one there as company.

He didn't like to be this way
He shut his eyes and dreamed back.

Back to floating on the surface of the water,
Back to being whole
Waiting for someone to get him out.
That someone never came.

He didn't like to be this way
He shut his eyes and dreamed back.

Back to being under everyone's feet
At the bottom of a ship
With nothing left to eat.
He dies, dies.

He didn't like to be this way
He shut his eyes and dreamed back.

Back to fighting on an unknown ship
He kills a man with a patch for an eye
The captain of the ship attacks him.
He is defeated and captured.

He didn't like to be this way
He shut his eyes and dreamed back.

Standing at the bow of a ship
Looking out over the sea
This is his own ship
Sailing the seas he knows.

He liked to be this way
He shut his eyes and dreamed hard to stay there.

Jessica Mulholland (12)
Methodist College

The Football

(Inspired by 'Fishbones Dreaming' by Matthew Sweeney)

I, the football lay there, in the bin,
no longer being played with,
in day or dim.

No more football,
No more games,
Thinking back, I remember,

Lying, impaled on a thorn bush,
air seeping out.
Turning into mush.

No more football,
No more games,
Thinking back, I remember,

The last few matches, goals and the net,
6-2, 5-4, 2-1 or 5-0,
they always won, I would bet.

No more football,
No more games,
Thinking back, I remember,

The very first kick, in, off the post.
What a goal!
But they would never boast.

No more football,
No more games,
Thinking back, I remember,

Sitting on the shelf, in the shop,
then picked up by a child.
He never knew I'd be a flop,

Once more I wish I could be alive,
being played with again.
Just one more chance not to be in the bin.

Ben Lowry (12)
Methodist College

Memories

(Inspired by 'Fishbones Dreaming' by Matthew Sweeney)

Skeleton Bones, lay on the sand bed.
She was a normal eight-year-old girl.
Nothing is down there to keep her company
But sands.

She didn't like to be this way.
She looked back . . .

Back to when, with a splash,
The sack went down, down and down.
With her delicate body in the sack,
Not breathing or moving.

She didn't like to be this way.
She looked back . . .

Back to when her cold body
Got stuffed into a dirty, old sack,
Put her body into the boot,
And went for a ride.

She didn't like to be this way.
She looked back . . .

Back to when the last words were,
'I hate you so much!'
Got pushed down the stairs,
Rolled, rolled and snapped
By her stepmum.

She didn't like to be this way.
She looked back . . .

Back to when Mum and Dad had an argument.
Dad shouting and Mum crying.
The next day from then on
Never saw Mum again.

She didn't like to be this way.
She looked back . . .

Back to when she was little,
In the park, with Mum and Dad.
Holding her hands and laughing together.
When they didn't know what the word 'sad' meant.

She liked to be that way.
She dreamed hard to try and stay there.

Hee Jin Cho (14)
Methodist College

Skeleton On The Seabed

(Inspired by 'Fishbones Dreaming' by Matthew Sweeney)

Lying on the seabed,
Only company are fish,
Wet blackness is surrounding,
In his cabin on the ship.

He remembers, swimming in his room,
As water rose around him
And remembers people on deck
Shouting as the ship started to sink.

He remembers journeys on the ship,
A different country every other day.
Different faces, friendly and not.
Only stayed a few nights, then sailed away.

He remembers, hard times in stormy weather,
Trying to help to stay afloat.
Pulling on ropes and climbing the mast.
He'd done it times before and thought they could cope.

Now all of his efforts seemed to be wasted
To then lie on the seabed.
He turns to talk to his mates in the cabin,
He remembers, he is dead.

Ciara McGlade (12)
Methodist College

Through The Window

Ahead I see an old barren runway,
Where war planes used to fly.
A busy road to the left,
Where cars go whizzing by.

The barley is cut by a combine harvester,
On a bright summer's day
And once a year a shot goes off
To signal the start of May.

I often see a little yacht,
Drifting across Lough Neagh,
And farmers walking with their hunting dogs
So I watch as they look for their prey.

Across the waters I can see,
A far and distant town,
But in the fog and mist,
There's only the Mourne Mountains of County Down.

Eimeár McGarry (15)
Methodist College

The Girl On The Hockey Pitch

She was standing at the end of the pitch.
Stick in both hands.
Ready in case she got passed the ball, by any small chance.
It was in the midfielder's possession, moving along the gravel.
With one little tap she could get the ball
And head for the goals as she travelled.
And the ball was passed and she received,
But she was stopped in her tracks by a defender who seemed
                                               to be pleased.
But it wasn't over yet, they were still both fighting for the ball.
She went one way, then the next and got her glory back from
                                               the dodge.
She ran and ran. She was in the circle, she was on a roll.
She was nearly there, she was there and then she scored her goal.

Morgan MacIntyre (12)
Methodist College

It's A Cat's Life!

Born, so petite and helpless,
Stretching limbs and tiny claws.
Screwed up eyes and little chirrups
Of bliss or sadness, who's to know?

A little older, a little bolder,
Never ceasing kitten tricks.
Big round eyes, so innocent, yet wicked,
A growing appetite with each lick.

A big strong Tom now,
He brings birdies as presents for me.
He's macho and cunning,
But when the light goes out he's a purring softie.

Growing older and broader,
A lap cat's the job.
He yawns, eats and purrs,
And never worries at all.

He can't do a lot now,
Yet he's lovely each day.
Gives us all sadness after our happiness
When he passes away.

Juliet Stirling (13)
Methodist College

Polar Bear

He needs . . .
Teeth like sharp kitchen knives,
Ears like a teddy bear's ears but large and white,
Fur like Christmas time snow,
Tail like a rabbit's tail but white and large,
And last but not least a roar like a lion's roar.

Maurizio Liberante (11)
Methodist College

Dream Stream

One night when I couldn't sleep,
I decided to take a little peep,
Into other people's dreams,
So I jumped into the dream stream.

First I came to my friend's dream,
She dreamt about a monstrous scream,
That kept coming from a bay.
I got scared so I hurried away.

In the dream stream I found the butcher's,
But it was boring so I moved onto the teacher's
She dreamt that my class was good,
Getting on with our work, as we should.

I felt like a good scare,
So I went to find a nightmare.
But when the monster appeared from its bed,
It looked at me and turned and fled.

I went too, really annoyed,
So I decided nightmares were something to avoid.
I had a look but the dreams were boring,
And then I heard someone snoring.

Suddenly sleep came to me,
So I chose a dream by the sea.
I jumped into a pea-green boat,
And away I did float . . .

Kirsty Kee (12)
Methodist College

Dinosaur Bones

(Inspired by 'Fishbones Dreaming' by Matthew Sweeney)

Dinosaur bones lay in the museum, all polished.
He was a full skeleton, every piece.
How did he get this way?

He didn't really like
All the people staring.
He thought back . . .

Back to when he was fossilised and
Lost in the million years gone by.
He thought back . . .

Back to when he was lying on the grass
With many veloceraptors ripping him to shreds.
He thought back . . .

Back to when he was in a fight with a
Larger dinosaur than himself.
He thought back . . .

Back to when the lights filled the night sky
And the birds soared over the Jurassic plains.
There's no need to think back now.

He's found his home,
With his son and family
Instead of being alone.

He thought back . . .

Adam Irwin (12)
Methodist College

Dinosaur

(Inspired by 'Fishbones Dreaming' by Matthew Sweeney)

Dinosaur stood in London museum,
he was a full skeleton, all polished,
soon Jurassic Park would be in for him.

He didn't like people taking photos
and watching in amazement,
he tried to dream back.

Back to when he was in the ground,
he'd been there for millions of years and then
suddenly an archaeologist was about to dig him up.

He didn't like to be this way,
He tried to dream back.

Back to when he had flesh
and was the colour of grass
and a T-Rex was about to dig into dinner!

He didn't like to be this way,
He tried to dream back.

Back to when he was about to drink the cool spring water,
And he got a glimpse of fate,
A dinosaur about to pounce,
He was scared.

He didn't like to be this way,
He tried to dream back.

Back to when he was witnessing his child's birth,
a miniature of him,
seeing the world for the first time
and gazing up at him.

He loved to be this way,
He never wants to dream back.

Jonathan Stanfield (13)
Methodist College

In The Dust

(Inspired by 'Fishbones Dreaming' by Matthew Sweeney)

As the eerie silence filled the graveyard,
I was no longer a fat pot of lard,
I'd turned into dust and dust I remain,
In the searing desert of my life's great pain.

The sand in the desert whirled around,
I shut my eyes and thought back.

Back to the time when the plane crashed,
Into the base my plane was smashed,
Not much sooner did the flames leer,
Coming to me as quick as lightning tear.

The wind blew me so cold that I shivered,
I closed my eyes and thought back.

Back to the time I was safe in the plane,
Fell out of my eyes, tears of sad pain,
Knowing I'll never see my wife,
This way I was forced to end my life.

A wind blew me so cold that I shivered,
I closed my eyes and thought back.

Back to the time I held the post,
As I read the letter my body froze,
I would never tell my loving wife,
I didn't want to put her in strife.

A wind blew me so cold that I shivered,
I closed my eyes and thought back.

Back to the time I played with my son,
In football, two goals he had done,
My wife clapped and cheered at the back,
I lost to him, my skills were at lack.

The wind felt pleasantly warm,
I shut my eyes tight and dreamed on.

Nathan Jun (13)
Methodist College

Skeleton Bones

(Inspired by 'Fishbones Dreaming' by Matthew Sweeney)

Skeleton Bones lay on the seabed
He was a head, arms and ribs
Skeleton Bones was a human, been dead for 35 years.

Being this way was lonely
He thought back in his life

Back to when he was on the ship
He was frightened when he heard the announcement
The announcement saying, 'Life jackets on,' but
Skeleton Bones didn't put it on.

Being this way was scary
He thought back in his life

Back to when he was happy dancing the night away
With his wife, two children, his family
Music playing, pop and rock, all sorts!
Some his favourites.

Being this way was fabulous
He thought back again, for more happy times.

Back to when he was at home in his warm bed
Brown hair and blue eyes
With his family safe and warm
No one could take this feeling of happiness away.

Skeleton Bones just lay there
Soggy skin and eye sockets empty
He was alone, again
He wondered what his family was doing now, dead or alive?
He wished he had that orange life jacket to save him . . .

Kym Irwin (12)
Methodist College

Coco The Coconut!

(Inspired by 'Fishbones Dreaming' by Matthew Sweeney)

Coco the coconut sat in the bin
Well, really what was left of him.
Soon the bin men would come
Then he really would be done.

He didn't like to be this way
He shut his eyes and tried to think back.

Back to when he was sitting in the middle of the table,
The family crowded around him,
The mother raised the knife and . . .

He didn't like to be this way
He shut his eyes and tried to think back.

Back to when he was sitting on the shore
When the little boy picked him up.
He was carried away and heard the boy shout, 'Score!'

He didn't like to be this way
He shut his eyes and tried to think back.

Back to when he was floating on the sea
Taken away from his family
The waves splashing,
The tide crashing.

He didn't like to be this way
He shut his eyes and tried to think back.

Back to when he was swaying in the breeze
Surrounded by his fellow coconuts
The Jamaican music booming below
The swinging rhythm flow.

He liked to be this way
And as the bin men took him away
He closed his eyes and tried to think back.

Lorna Hamilton (12)
Methodist College

Autumn

Golden sunshine shines down
Through the falling leaves
As they spin, floating down
Falling on the pile.

Children run through the forest
In hats, scarves and welly boots.
Kicking leaves up in the air
And stuffing them down each other's necks.

Hedgehogs bury under leaf piles
To settle down for winter.
Squirrels collect acorns
Gathering for their harvest.

As night falls, the fireworks start exploding,
Luminous in the dark sky.
Sparkling as they fall
Showering us with light.

Elizabeth Crooks (13)
Methodist College

Crocodile

Selected items:
teeth,
how he moves,
where he stays,
body and personality

He needs teeth like shining, jagged rocks,
He gallops like a great stallion,
He swims through the swamp as silent as a mouse,
His body is like a long, scaly bulldog.
He will brutally tear his prey apart.

Adam Carr (11)
Methodist College

The Nut

(Inspired by 'Fishbones Dreaming' by Matthew Sweeney)

I lay there on the path
All smashed and broken,
Because of the young ones' games.

I didn't like to be this way,
I shut my eyes and dreamt back . . .

Back to when I was on a string
Hitting others hard and fast.
Making them crack and scream,
Until I finally got broken.

I didn't like to be this way,
I shut my eyes and dreamt back . . .

Back to when I was being soaked in vinegar
Before being toasted
Then getting string tied to me.

I didn't like to be this way,
I shut my eyes and dreamt back . . .

Back to when I was on the ground
Under the tree with my friends,
With children coming and picking
Us up to take to their homes.

I didn't like to be this way,
I shut my eyes and dreamt back . . .

Back to when I was in the tree
With everybody around me.
In the shade under the leaves.

I liked to be that way
I dreamt hard to try and stay there.

Connell Stewart (12)
Methodist College

The Fall

The fall brings fallen leaves
the trees stand tragically by
powerless to prise the leaves
from their falling doom.

The leaves look up
the trees look down
and in-between them
a herd of heavy children.

Cold trees cry out
against autumn's anger
wanting to wear their natural coats
now lying down below.

As the months melt by
the fall flies away
and as spring spreads around
the giants gulp down its taste.

Brajith Srigengan (13)
Methodist College

Statue Of The Infant Jesus

A glorious crown - jewel encrusted
With diamonds divine and humble rubies
Sparkles golden in the light
From its place on the window's ledge.

Below peeks the head of a boy
Strained by his humble crown
And smothered in his gold-encrusted dress.
There he stands - sacred.

His baby eyes remain fixed
Hopeful, peaceful, jubilant
But forever watching.
Watching and judging me.

Steve Heagney (15)
Methodist College

The Corrupted View From My Window

Trees, hills and houses scattered around,
Lakes, sea, boats to carry you far away.
To the left, the old witch next door
Hanging out her washing.
Pink, frilly knickers
Grand airs she doesn't deserve.
I am isolated.

I can see my mum climbing the mountain,
She is in Manchester, but I am in Belfast.
Sometimes I forget that she is gone,
But I remember before I would like to.

There's a ladybird crawling on my window,
One of many found in the summer.
They are so small and insignificant,
Like me really.

I can see my best friends over the mountains,
Over the sea, in another world,
And I feel alone.

Helen Moore (15)
Methodist College

How To Make A Mouse . . .

She needs . . .
A long, thin tail like a snake,
Soft fur like velvet,
Short legs like a millipede for running,
Small body that looks like a plum,
And long whiskers like a caterpillar for feeling,
Deep brown eyes like mud for seeing things
                        that are far away.

Emily Cheung (12)
Methodist College

Bully For You

You've all heard the story that ends with a rope,
A young boy takes his life when he's lost all hope.
But do not be fooled by the blood and the tears,
There's much more deep down than at first there appears.

Did she not have time to hear her son's silent cries,
To capture the torment displayed in his eyes.
The Devil's got her number, she's lost her son,
Where now can she hide? To where will she run?

The time has come, he knows what to do,
Your torment is over, well bully for you.

Now look at that boy, look into his face
And then you can see that Hell's a real place.
Should you feel angry or sad or afraid?
Feel what you wish, the price had to be paid.
For eyes can deceive, and ears they can lie
When they hear the soft tones of a mother's cry.

But to find out the truth, to see why they're in last
To work out the future, you must look to the past.

Graham Richardson (16)
Methodist College

Pursuit

He moves through the water as swift as a cheetah,
A predator fast on his trail.
His scales are shining like bright stars.
A beacon for all to see.

The reef lies ahead,
Its nooks and crannies a place of sanctuary,
Just reached in time.
He can rest now, safe from danger.

Alanna Holmes (11)
Methodist College

Nature

Far off in the distance, the lough it stands alone,
Captivated by the sunlight, in its multicoloured tone.
The red, purple and orange creep past night's dark gaze
And meet fellow elements to create a liquidy haze.

The dew's tender touch illuminates a masterpiece,
While its creator finishes off an insignificant life, a very unlucky beast.
Its senses become alert, it stands unduly on guard
The eight spindly legs contract and move, leaving its victim
mercilessly scarred.

The great red beast trots past, his majesty assured,
His long and drawn-out fast is now as good as cured.
The brace of young rabbits moved in nought but a night,
Will not live through this gruesome fight.

I look out through my window, and this is what I see
Nature will not have listened to those with greatest plea
But instead it gives to whom, who can call upon its strength,
They who have proven, they're on evolution's superior wavelength.

Mark McCauley (16)
Methodist College

How To Make A Rabbit

Selected parts - ears, eyes, feet, fur and teeth

He needs . . .
Long ears that droop like dead flowers,
Eyes as round as clocks,
Feet as springy as a kangaroo's,
Velvety fur that feels as soft as silk
And teeth as hard as nails
To chomp through carrots with.

Rachel Watters (12)
Methodist College

The Mouse

Whiskers as thin as a single hair,
Nose as pink as lipstick,
Eyes as brown and deep as a pit,
Legs as short as a door handle,
Ears as round as oranges,
Body as small as a mango,
Colour as grey as tarmac.

Holly Graham (11)
Methodist College

Friend Or Foe

M oving so quietly like a thief in our house,
O ur squeaky friend is a little white mouse.
U ntil he gets some food to eat
S tealthily he'll run upon his feet.
E veryone's scared to leave their seat.

Philip Stewart (12)
Methodist College

Dragon

He needs wings like a giant vampire bat,
He needs horns like a rampaging buffalo,
He needs a tail as sharp as an eagle's eyesight,
He needs spines like those of a lizard,
And a tongue like a snake's
Mildly scorched by a breath of flame.

Oliver Dickson (11)
Methodist College

The Gazelle

The gazelle, an elegant and graceful creature,
She moves swiftly away from an advancing cheetah.
Bouncing up and down on her four stiff legs.
Her horns long and curved, like a gleaming cutlass,
Avoiding tall grass where her enemies hide.
Her prancing gait suddenly shows her fear,
The scent of the cheetah is not far away.
The chase begins, her flight takes place,
Death is near!

Olivia Lowry (11)
Methodist College

The Tiger

T he tiger quietly stalks his prey.
I nvisible in the undergrowth,
G radually he sneaks up on his prey,
E erily quiet like a master burglar.
R apidly, like lightning, he pounces.

Karl Hudson (11)
Methodist College

Yeti

Hair like a warm fuzzy coat,
Toenails as long as icicles,
Horns like a bull,
Eyes as piercing as spears on fire
And a call as raging and loud as the wolf's.

Conor Cathcart (11)
Methodist College

How To Make A Spider

He needs . . .
Big, long, fast legs like a cheetah's,
Long and pointy fangs like spikes,
Poison coming out of his fangs like a waterfall,
Eyes like bright red lights,
And short fine hairs all over his body.

Conner Gallagher (12)
Methodist College

Hallowe'en

Hallowe'en is here,
People start to cheer.
The dogs start to bark,
As the fireworks start to spark.

All the children get dressed up,
As they wait to get punked up.
The witches start to wake,
The ground starts to shake.

As the ground starts to shake,
The bats start to wake,
And as the bats start to wake,
The witches start to make a creepy poison potion,
That will make the vampires scream.

You hear the witches laughing,
You hear the vampires stretching.
You see the children laughing,
As they see the fireworks gleaming.

Now Hallowe'en is here I jump and shout and cheer,
As I hope I get some fear.

Oh I love Hallowe'en
I wish it was here for a long time this year.

Danielle Martin (13)
Orangefield High School

Hallowe'en

H allowe'en is here.
A ll the children are trick or treating
L ights are getting lit
L aughing is heard of the children
O thers are setting up the food
W indows are decorated
E veryone is scared
E veryone is lighting fireworks
N ight falls and Hallowe'en is over.

Sarah-Louise McLaughlin (12)
Orangefield High School

A Friend

A friend is someone who is always there.
A friend will play with you when others won't.
A friend will always care.
A friend does not leave you alone.
A friend when not at their own, they'll be at your home
Friends will never let you down.
A true friend is a friend for life.

Adam Bradford (13)
Orangefield High School

Football

F avourite team is Man United.
O ff the pitch if you get a red card.
O n as a sub, be clapped by the crowd.
T eams good, teams bad, all still play.
B ottom of the table, need to win some matches.
A sport for all to play.
L osing is bad and winning is good.
L eaving home to play away.

Wayne Brown (12)
Orangefield High School

Fashion

As I prance down the street in my new clothes
    I am so looking my best.
I feel so good and so, so fresh.
    I wear a pair of jeans and a pink top
this is enough to make anyone stop.

I feel like I'm a pop star in my new cloths
    who would stand and give a little pose.
I am looking great in my casual wear
    what if I get dirty oh, it's too much to bear.

My feet are killing, I can't wait to go
    I missed my bus, oh no! No! No!
I call for a taxi, it comes right away,
    I am never wearing those shoes again,
        never again, no way!

Cory McCaw (13)
Orangefield High School

Summertime

Summertime is cool,
You get off school.
Summertime is bright and sunny,
You can do things that are really funny.

Summertime is a great time of year,
You get to run around with your friends and cheer.
Summertime lasts only a short while,
So hurry up and get out for a while.

Aaron Ashton (12)
Orangefield High School

This Is How I Feel About You

Love is a feeling of warmth inside
A night by the sweet, gentle breeze.
Love is a feeling I have inside
This is how I feel about you.

Love is a feeling that lasts forever
It makes me warm and happy.
Love is a feeling that takes a while,
This is how I feel about you.

Love is a feeling that I long to keep
It makes me feel so special.
Love is a feeling that can tear you apart
This is how I feel about you.

Love is a feeling that shouldn't be messed with
It can lead to broken hearts.
Love is a feeling you can't live without
This is how I feel about you.

Leah Reid (14)
Orangefield High School

Christmas

As Christmas creeps up the nights get longer
and the roads get louder with cars.
When Christmas creeps up, shops get filled with gifts
that can only be bought at Christmas.
The streets get brighter with lights and over-decorated houses.
When Christmas creeps up people get more excited
and make it seem longer by thinking of it all the time.
I wish Christmas would not creep up, I want it to rush up.

John Miller (14)
Orangefield High School

Hallowe'en

H appy Hallowe'en to all the people out there getting ready
A ll the little children go out trick or treating in their scary
    little costumes.
L ate at night the wind blows and creatures start to appear!
L ong sticks of candy which are being eaten in one minute
    by hungry little kids.
O ld people jump when the fireworks go . . . *bang!*
W itches flying high in the sky looking for people who they can scare.
E verybody jumps at the sign of something scary!
E ven the little animals who are scared run for shelter.
N ow Hallowe'en is over and the vampires are getting hungry,
    so would you please put some of your blood in the vampire's
    old mouth?

Stacey McNeice (12)
Orangefield High School

Hallowe'en

H is for Hallowe'en parties, how much fun is this?
A is for all the fun and games.
L is for laughter, it is all you can hear.
L is for how much louder and louder this laughter gets.
O is for oh, what a noise.
W is for what a cool costume you have.
E is for everyone out trick and treating.
E is for everyone dressed up as ghosts, goblins, devils and more.
N is for now it is midnight, everyone is indoors,
    it is all quiet again for another year.

Danielle Mudd (12)
Orangefield High School

My Year

January - cold and just started back to school from the Christmas break and can't wait to show off all my new, cool stuff.

February - the month of love, St Valentine's Day. Everyone is trying to guess their secret admirer.

March - the start of spring and the leaves on the trees are starting to grow again.

April - the Easter bunnies are out to play and everyone is so full up because of all the chocolate from the Easter eggs.

May - May Day, we get off school, something to look forward to, but we do our horrible exams.

June - one month to go until we are off school for the summer, everyone is so excited!

July - it's hot and everyone is getting out their buckets and spades to go on holiday.

August - people going down to the beach to soak up the last of the sunshine.

September - back to school to start a new year at school. How boring!

October - The month of fireworks and people out trick or treating for Hallowe'en. Boo!

November - Children In Need month, everyone raising money for charity and having a laugh.

December - Christmas is here all over again and getting lots of presents. Then we have New Year's Eve for the whole year to start over again.

Nicola McNeill (14)
Orangefield High School

Belfast Troubles

We spent many cold nights
Squeezed tightly together,
Blast bombs and petrol bombs
Exploding like dangerous fireworks.

Bodies broken, houses burned,
Bottles and stones flying
Like a swarm of huge
And deadly insects.

Fire engines, police cars,
Ambulances screaming through the night,
Like demented banshees.

Gary Wright (15)
Orangefield High School

Hallowe'en

Hallowe'en is near
So watch out my dear.

As you may get a fright
While you are sleeping at night.

There's all sorts of monsters and creatures wouldn't you know
But watch out, when they go.

Keep your eyes open and beware
And if they come, stick up for yourself, if you dare.

On Hallowe'en night, stay in your bed
They will try to get your sweets, but they would prefer you instead.

Sophia Patton (12)
Orangefield High School

The Perfect Teacher

Begin with a bag full of sweetness
Stir in a pound full of kindness
Mix in rosy-red cheeks
Add a beautiful smile
Next stir in lovely hazel eyes
A pinch of beauty
Add a jug of laughter
A bowl full of love to share with everyone
Pour in a cheerful voice
Then put it into the oven for an hour
Serve with a name of . . .
    Mrs Wilson.

Rhiann McWhirter (13)
Orangefield High School

My Mum

Begin with a bag full of *love,*
This will make the mixture of *kindness.*
Add a teaspoon of *friendship*
And an ounce of *smiles,*
Mix with *hugs and kisses*
For added *motherly advice.*
Next, stir in *generosity*
Or *caring knowledge.*
In order to be *helpful,*
Bake for your mother dearest
And serve with all the love and goodness in your heart.

Amanda Conlane (13)
Orangefield High School

Our Lack Of Understanding

So many things happen in life,
So much pain, so much strife,
No one can give definite reasons
For the constant loss during the seasons.

Although people try to understand,
Why people 'disappear' from our land,
The questions are, every day, expanding,
Along with our lack of understanding.

So much effort for just one soul,
To carry on and accept life's toll,
And when it comes our time to leave,
Friends and loved ones can only grieve.

Why are we born, to soon be gone?
Why do we have to carry on?
Passing through life one by one,
At certain times both old and young.

At the end, all the pain will cease,
Your body will finally find a release.
Everything past has been said and done
And everyone will meet when our time has come.

Maria Doherty (17)
Our Lady Of Mercy Girls' School